slow-cooked
comfort

also by
LYDIE MARSHALL

a passion for my provence
a passion for potatoes
soup of the day
cooking with lydie marshall

slow-cooked comfort

LYDIE MARSHALL

soul-satisfying stews, casseroles, and braises for every occasion

HarperCollins*Publishers*

HarperCollins books may be purchased for educational, business, or sales promotional use. For information, please write: Special Markets Department, HarperCollins Publishers, 10 East 53rd Street, New York, NY 10022.

FIRST EDITION

DESIGNED BY PH.D, WWW.PHDLA.COM

Printed on acid-free paper

Library of Congress Cataloging-in-Publication Data

Marshall, Lydie.
Slow-cooked comfort : soul-satisfying stews, casseroles, and braises for every occasion / Lydie Marshall.
—1st ed.
p. cm.
ISBN-10: 0-06-058042-9
ISBN-13: 978-0-06-058042-1
1. Electric cookery, Slow. I. Title.

TX827.M37 2005
641.5'884—dc22   2005040367

05 06 07 08 09 ❖/RRD 10 9 8 7 6 5 4 3 2 1

TO THE MEMORY OF richard
olney

acknowledgments

To all my friends, a big thank-you for all your help testing and criticizing all the recipes in this book and sharing your own recipes with me: Neil and Lorna Myers, Judy and Norman Stein, Sarah Lambert, Mary Beth Boland, Steffen Andrews, Patricia Fieldsteel, Tara Reddi, Jim Groff, Amanda Berman, Betty Zucker, Viviana Carbollo, Karen Hanson, Heather and Steve Walker. I can't forget my two faithful helpers, Arlette Vantrebout and Françoise Surrugue, *Je vous remercie de tout mon cœur*. Without Susan Friedland, my editor and friend, this book would not have been written. Thank you, Susan!

contents

intro
du

o-
ction

This book is dedicated to the late Richard Olney, who taught me the principles of good cooking. Living in New York in the 1960s, I'd wait impatiently every month for my copy of the magazine *Cuisine et Vins de France* in order to read Richard's column *Un Américain Gourmand à Paris.* Then I'd cook his menu for my own family. Later, in the 1970s, when Richard published his menus in English as *The French Menu Cookbook,* he produced what is still a classic for everybody interested in the techniques of good cooking.

I had watched my mother cook when I was a child in Paris, during World War II. Later, in Cleveland with my aunt, who had married an American, I learned a good deal more. It was through reading and re-creating most of Richard's menus for my family, however, that I really acquired the fundamentals of good cooking. That's why, when my editor, Susan Friedland, asked me to write a book on braising, I thought immediately of Richard. I remembered how he loved stews and casseroles, which he called simple food, as much as the more complicated dishes for which he was better-known.

In this book I address three closely related dishes: stews, braises, and casseroles. All three make use of economical ingredients, almost always using the cheaper cuts of meat and rarely requiring exotic or expensive additions. Also, most of them are slow-cooked and reheatable, making them ideal for busy folks who like to entertain but don't have the time or staff for complicated, last-minute preparations.

When preparing a meat stew, look for the cheaper cuts of meat. But these cuts need to cook in moist heat, in a pot with a tight-fitting lid, and be treated with tender care to preserve all their flavors.

Cooking meat in moist heat was very popular on the farms of Europe. A *brasier*, a culinary word of French origin, described a bed of coals (*les braises*) in which a crockery or cast-iron pot was tightly closed and buried in the large fireplace of a farm kitchen. The pot was usually left in the fireplace overnight to achieve a long tenderizing process for tough cuts of meat like beef rump or shank. Game was also very popular and needed long braising to make it tender and flavorful.

Certainly, nothing is more wonderful than to come into a kitchen where there is a pot on the stove or in the oven, with a stew cooking away for several hours! I recall fondly the day I made a lamb stew with my students in my New York brownstone. That was the day when Mimi Sheraton, then food editor of the *New York Times*, who was writing a critique of all fifty-two cooking schools in the city, was scheduled to visit my class. The delicious aroma of lamb stew engulfed the hallway and the kitchen. The moment she entered, she stopped, turned to me and announced, "Well! This is the best-smelling cooking school I've been to!" When the list of cooking schools was published, there I was, on the centerfold of the *Times*, over the caption, "a no-nonsense school that is the best in town."

The techniques of stews and braises are simple; anyone who pays just a bit of attention to the cooking can produce excellent meals.

Today, *braising* is an umbrella word for a cooking technique in which meat or fowl is simmered in liquid with vegetables. Stews, daubes, ragouts, and fricassees are all braises. Sometimes the stew takes its name from the clay utensil in which it was originally cooked: a daube, a tagine. There is little difference between braising and stewing. Braised meat is kept whole and is moistened with less liquid than a stew. For example, a pot roast is a braise, whereas a stew is a braise of smaller pieces of meat and vegetables.

When stews are simmered in liquid on top of the stove, the liquid should bubble gently to the surface, never standing still. Escoffier, the well-known nineteenth-century French chef, called this gentle bubbling "a boil without a boil" *(Ça bout sans bouillir)*. Now and then, peek into the pot while the dish is cooking and let the condensation under the lid fall back into the pot. It's also a good idea to cover the meat with a buttered or oiled piece of parchment paper to keep it moist, even if the pot has a tight-fitting lid. Once the meat is cooked, depending on the cut, remove as much of the fat and impurities from the braising juices as possible. This will thicken the juices and transform them into a beautiful shiny sauce.

Strain the cooked meat or fowl over the pot; then transfer it to a heated serving dish if you are eating the stew immediately or put it in a container for later (in general, stews are better reheated). Move the pot off-center on the burner and raise the heat to a gentle boil. Now and then, skim off any fat that rises on the side of the pot not directly over the heat. Wait long enough for a skin to form on top of the fat and remove it along with the fat. You can do this with either a long-handled spoon or a soup spoon. Don't worry if you remove some of the sauce with it, or if there is a bit of fat left in the sauce. As it cooks, the sauce will gradually thicken and become shiny. If the stew is prepared ahead of time, refrigerate the meat and the sauce separately.

For some of the stews braised in the oven, I use an old technique, going back to when most stews were prepared in the embers of a fireplace, of sealing the lid and pot with a paste of flour and water. It's great because there is no need to stay in the house while the meat is cooking. Of course, if you don't want to bother with this paste, you can also peek into the pot occasionally and add a bit of water to compensate for escaped steam.

To make the paste, in a small mixing bowl gradually blend about $1/2$ cup of water into $1^1/2$ cups flour with the back of a fork until the flour is moistened. Use your fist to knead the mixture until it forms a ball the consistency of play-dough. The dough should be malleable but should not stick to your fingers. Brush the edges of the lid and the upper part of the pot with water. Tear off about 1 tablespoon of dough at a time and, with your fingers, flatten and stretch it into a piece roughly 4 inches long and 1 inch wide. Place it on the lid, pressing it into the space between the pot and the lid. Continue sealing the pot in this manner, overlapping the dough somewhat (the dough does shrink). Be sure to seal around the handles of the pot.

Today we cook stews in a heavy enameled cast-iron pot, called a Dutch oven or casserole, with a tight-fitting lid. Over the years, I have acquired Dutch ovens in many sizes, and I really think I've used them all in testing the recipes for this book. You don't need all these pots; improvise with your own cooking utensils as long as they are sturdy. For example, a cast-iron skillet is fine, but you might need to improvise a lid, and you can't store cooked food in it. When you wash cast iron, dry it immediately with paper towels and then rub with wax paper to keep it seasoned. I learned this trick from a student.

Casseroles, like stews, are heartwarming dishes, but elusive to define. Irma Rombauer, in *Joy of Cooking*, explains that in America a casserole means both the cooking vessel and the food prepared in it. I was a fifteen-year-old French girl when I came to live in Cleveland, Ohio. To welcome me to the neighborhood, our friendly next-door neighbor told my aunt that she was bringing us a casserole. I was perplexed. What strange customs Americans had! Why did my aunt need another pot in her kitchen? The mystery was quickly solved when I saw our neighbor arrive carrying her fragrant, delicious casserole (*gratin* in my mind). Casseroles are generally a mixture of several foods cooked and served in an ovenproof baking dish, often with a gratinéed top. Casseroles range from the humble and uncomplicated to elaborate dishes such as cassoulet or paella.

When a stew or a casserole is on my menu, there is always a tossed green salad afterward to complement it. Bon appétit!

slow-cooked
comfort

basics

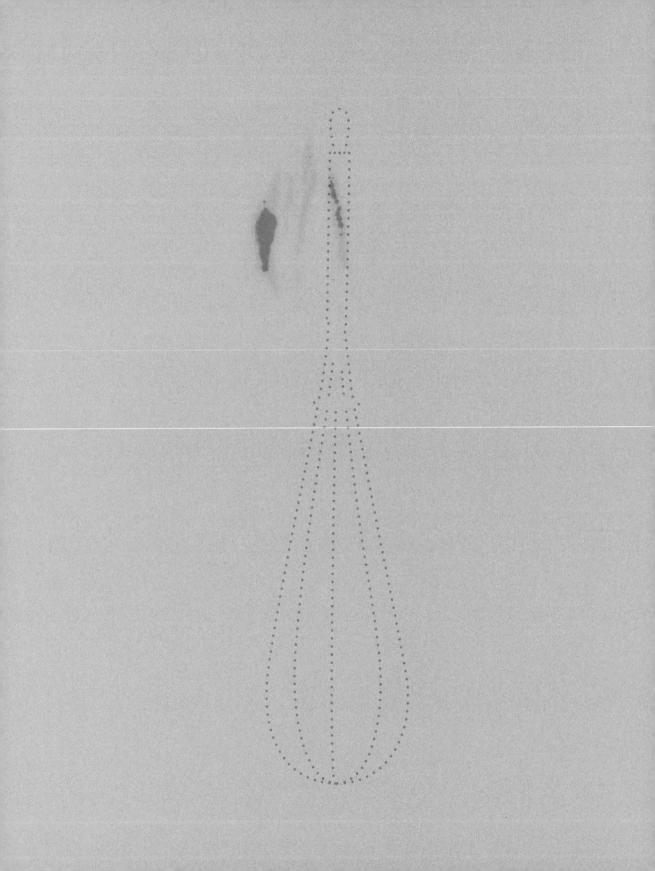

The kitchen is my favorite room in the house because it is where I do what I like to do best: cook for my family and friends. If you have a few basics in your pantry, refrigerator, or freezer, it's easy to make these recipes.

I make chicken stock all year long, bottle it, and freeze it until I need it. In the fall and winter, I prepare pot-au-feu, which makes a super beef stock for stews.

The recipe for homemade noodles is American; it's a soft dough made with a mixture of cake flour and unbleached flour, eggs, and cream—perfect for lasagna or ravioli.

I also always have prunes marinating in port, in a mason jar that I keep in the refrigerator. These are great served with meats and fowl, and they're also useful for ice cream and chocolate desserts.

It takes no time to make pastry dough in the food processor; I usually do several batches at a time, freeze the lot, and easily roll out a batch for a potpie whenever I feel like one.

And, voilà, I'm ready to cook.

braise of lamb shanks with garlic

This is the simplest preparation I know: lamb, garlic, water, and seasonings.

The number of garlic cloves is up to you. They are delicious mashed into the braising liquid. Remember to remove the germ of each clove if the garlic is over 3 months old.

2 tablespoons olive oil
4 lamb shanks (about 1 pound each)
8 large garlic cloves, peeled
1 teaspoon salt
Freshly ground black pepper

SERVES 4

In a 7$\frac{1}{4}$-quart Dutch oven, heat 2 tablespoons olive oil over medium heat. Brown the shanks evenly, turning them over frequently and adjusting the heat when necessary. This will take about 20 minutes.

Add the garlic and $\frac{1}{4}$ cup water. Season with salt and pepper. Cover tightly and braise over low heat for 1$\frac{1}{2}$ hours. Check the lamb now and then, making sure the water condensation on the underside of the lid falls back into the pan to create more cooking juices.

Transfer the shanks and half the garlic to a heated serving dish. Mash the remaining garlic into the cooking juices and serve alongside in a sauceboat.

lamb shanks braised in white wine

I love to go out to buy wine in Provence with my husband. I never know what we will discover—not just wines but perhaps an inspiration for a new dish. I was not disappointed the last time we went to Château des Tours, where we tasted a very nice fruity white wine. When we were ready to buy it, Christian Clauzel, the young winemaker, (without any prompting from me) wanted to share his recipe for his favorite lamb dish, braised in his own white wine. The next day, his lamb was the star of my dinner table.

SERVES 4

2 tablespoons olive oil
4 small lamb shanks (about 1 pound each), trimmed of all fat
1 teaspoon sugar
Salt
Freshly ground black pepper
4 medium carrots, peeled and cut into 1-inch slices
1 cup coarsely chopped onions
4 large cloves garlic, peeled
1 bottle (750 ml) white wine, preferably chardonnay
3 sprigs fresh thyme
1 bay leaf

Preheat the oven to 350 degrees.

Heat the oil in a 7^1/$_4$-quart Dutch oven over low to medium heat and brown the shanks evenly, turning them over occasionally, for about 20 minutes. Sprinkle with sugar, salt, and black pepper. When they are light gold in color, transfer them to a plate. Add the carrots, onions, and garlic to the pot and stir with a wooden spoon for 1 minute or so.

Return the shanks to the pot with the vegetables. Pour in the wine. Add the thyme and bay leaf. Cover. Seal the pot for braising in the oven, following the instructions on page xv, or see below.

Place the Dutch oven on the middle shelf of the oven and cook for at least 2 hours. If you did not seal the pot with the flour paste, check the lamb after 1 hour to see how fast the braising liquid is evaporating, and add more wine if necessary. At the end of the braising time, you should have 1 cup of cooking juices.

Transfer the shanks to a heated platter with the vegetables. Serve the cooking juices in a sauceboat.

leg of lamb à la provençale

In Provence, we buy boned shoulder of lamb for this dish, which is famous in Arles—Van Gogh country. In the United States, I make it with a boned leg of lamb; I ask the butcher to bone the lamb and cut it into 2 pieces—the shank part and the top part—so that it will fit into a Dutch oven.

2 tablespoons olive oil
4 pounds boned leg of lamb
Salt
Freshly ground pepper
4 large garlic cloves, not peeled
2 cups Tomato Sauce (page 6)
1 sprig fresh rosemary
1½ pounds Yukon Gold potatoes, peeled and cut into large cubes

SERVES
6 TO 8

In a 7¼-quart Dutch oven, heat the oil over medium heat and brown the meat on all sides. Season with salt and pepper.

Add the garlic cloves, tomato sauce, and rosemary and cover tightly.

Simmer the lamb and tomato sauce for 1 hour over medium-low heat. Now and then, uncover and let the condensation under the lid fall back into the pan; check the meat and stir it.

In a 4-quart pot, cover the potatoes with cold salted water and bring to a boil; lower the heat and cook half-covered for 10 minutes. When the potatoes are half-cooked, drain them in a colander set in the sink. Add the potatoes to the lamb for the last 15 minutes of cooking, or until the potatoes are tender.

Transfer the lamb to a large cutting board; cover loosely with foil and let stand 10 minutes before carving.

Serve with the tomato sauce in a sauceboat and the potatoes on the side.

the baker's wife's leg of lamb

Years ago, bakers' wives cooked dinner in the wood oven after their husbands had finished baking bread for the customers. While the oven cooled, several pots were put in for slow-cooking dishes. This dish of potatoes and lamb, a favorite of bakers' wives, was named for them. Nowadays, the leg of lamb is browned first and slowly baked over scalloped potatoes in a Dutch oven.

I do all the preparation ahead of time, but I cook the lamb just before serving. I find that the dish is not as moist when reheated as when freshly cooked.

Have the leg of lamb cut into the shank and the top of the leg. It will be easier to brown and fit into a Dutch oven.

**SERVES
6 TO 8**

1 small leg of lamb (about 6 pounds), split into shank and top of the leg
4 garlic cloves, peeled, each clove cut into eighths lengthwise
2 tablespoons olive oil
Salt
Freshly ground pepper
2 cups homemade or commercial chicken stock
3 pounds Yukon Gold or White Rose potatoes cut into 1/8-inch-thick slices
2/3 cup coarsely chopped onions or shallots
1 cup minced parsley

Trim all the fat off the lamb. With the point of a small kitchen knife, make deep incisions in the lamb and in them bury the slivers of garlic.

In a large skillet, heat the oil over medium heat. Brown the meat slowly, one piece at a time, turning it over once in a while and adjusting the heat (this will take about 15 minutes). Season with salt and freshly ground pepper. Transfer the leg onto a platter and reserve.

Discard the fat in the skillet and pour the chicken stock into the skillet. Bring the stock to a boil, scraping the bottom of the pan. Reserve.

Preheat the oven to 325 degrees.

Overlap 1/3 of the potato slices in 1 layer in a 7 1/4-quart Dutch oven. Sprinkle with salt and pepper, and cover with half the shallots or onions and half the parsley. Add a second layer of potatoes, season with salt and pepper, and cover with the remaining shallots or onions and parsley. Add the last layer of potatoes and season with salt and pepper.

Put the lamb on top of the potatoes. Strain in the reserved liquid and cover tightly. If you wish, seal the pot, following the instructions on page xv.

Bake the lamb in the middle of the oven for 1 1/2–2 hours. If you have not sealed the pot with flour paste, check the lamb after 1 hour; if the cooking juices are evaporating too fast, add more chicken stock. Don't let the potatoes dry out.

spring lamb stew

In France, it's called a navarin, and is made with shoulder of spring lamb; in the States I prefer to buy part of a leg, which is milder and less fatty than the shoulder. This recipe is also essential for the Cassoulet I make (page 76). The stew develops flavor when made 2 to 3 days ahead. Serve with Braise of Spring Vegetables (page 162).

SERVES 4

2 pounds boned leg of lamb, cut into 2-inch cubes
3 tablespoons flour
Salt
Freshly ground black pepper
2 tablespoons olive oil
1 teaspoon sugar
1 large onion, cut into eighths
4 carrots, cut into 2-inch-long pieces
1 tablespoon minced garlic
1 cup homemade or commercial chicken stock
1 large sprig of thyme

Pat the meat dry with paper towels.

Season the flour with a large pinch of salt and black pepper.

Heat 2 tablespoons olive oil in a large skillet. Dip the meat, a few pieces at a time, in the flour. Brown the meat in the oil, turning the pieces and sprinkling with sugar to caramelize the lamb. Transfer the meat to a 5$1/2$-quart Dutch oven.

Add the carrots, onion, and garlic to the skillet. With a wooden spoon, stir the vegetables until they color lightly (about 3 minutes).

Add the vegetables to the meat; sprinkle with salt and pepper. Pour in the chicken stock and add 1 large sprig of fresh thyme. Bring to a light boil, cover the Dutch oven, and simmer over medium-low heat for 1 hour or until the meat is tender. Now and then, uncover, let the steam under the lid fall back into the stew, and stir the meat.

Transfer the meat to a heated platter and cover with foil. To degrease the cooking juices, follow the directions on page xiv.

Ladle some of the sauce over the lamb and serve the remaining sauce in a sauceboat.

note

The stew can be prepared several days ahead. Refrigerate the meat and sauce separately. When you are nearly ready to eat, remove the fat congealed on top of the sauce and reheat the lamb.

lamb à la grecque

My Greek friends from Poulithra make this wonderful lamb casserole with rice. In the States, I prefer leg of lamb; it's less fatty than the shoulder traditionally used in Greece.

SERVES 4 TO 6

2½ pounds very lean boned leg of lamb, cut into 2-inch cubes
3 tablespoons lard or oil
2 teaspoons salt
Freshly ground black pepper
12 small white onions, peeled
1 14-ounce can Italian plum tomatoes, chopped
1 tablespoon paprika
3 cups homemade or commercial chicken stock
1 bay leaf
1 cup short-grain rice

Pat the meat dry with paper towels.

Heat 2 tablespoons lard in a large skillet over medium heat and brown the meat evenly, a few pieces at a time. Transfer the meat to a 3-quart ovenproof baking dish, and season with salt and pepper.

Add 1 tablespoon lard to the same skillet and gently sauté the small white onions over moderate heat for 2–3 minutes until lightly brown. Transfer to the baking dish with the meat.

Add the chopped tomatoes and tomato juice to the skillet, stirring for 1 minute over moderate heat. Season with paprika, salt, and pepper. Cover, lower the heat, and simmer for 10 minutes. Add to the meat.

Preheat the oven to 350 degrees.

Turn the heat to high under the skillet and pour in 2 cups stock, scraping the bottom of the pan and bringing the stock to a boil. Pour the boiling liquid over the meat, and cover with aluminum foil.

Bake in the middle of the oven for 1 hour.

Bring the remaining chicken stock to a boil and pour it over the rice. Add to the lamb, cover tightly, and bake for another 20 minutes or until the rice is fork-tender.

curry lamb stew

This curry lamb stew comes from Sumatra and Borneo, parts of the Malay Peninsula. It is one of those dishes that develop more flavor when cooked 1 or 2 days ahead of time.

SERVES 4

2 pounds very lean boned leg of lamb, cut into 2-inch cubes
2 tablespoons imported Indian curry, hot or mild (use according to taste)
2 teaspoons anise powder
2 teaspoons ground cinnamon
4 tablespoons vegetable or olive oil
4 cups coarsely chopped onions
Salt
1/4 teaspoon cayenne
1 medium carrot, cut into 1/4-inch slices
1 small red bell pepper, cut into 1/2-inch cubes
garlic
1 large Yukon Gold potato, cut into 1/2-inch cubes
2 garlic cloves, minced
1/2 cup unsweetened coconut milk

Preheat the oven to 325 degrees.

Pat the meat dry with paper towels. Reserve on a plate.

Mix the curry, anise, and cinnamon powders in a small bowl and reserve.

Heat 2 tablespoons oil in a large skillet over medium heat and brown the onions, stirring for 5 minutes. Transfer them to a deep 3-quart ovenproof casserole and reserve.

Add 1 tablespoon oil to the skillet and brown a few pieces of meat at a time, sprinkling with the spice mixture and salt. Put the meat on top of the onions.

Add 1 tablespoon oil to the skillet and brown the vegetables with the garlic for 3–4 minutes; season with more salt. Add the vegetables to the meat.

Pour the coconut milk over the meat and vegetables and cover tightly with aluminum foil.

Bake in the middle of the oven for 1 1/2 to 2 hours.

note

This stew can stay refrigerated for 2 to 3 days. Bring back to room temperature; then reheat in a 300-degree oven for 20 minutes or until hot.

lamb and bean stew

When I make this stew in summer, I cook it with fresh cranberry beans. I freeze shelled, raw cranberry beans for winter, but if I run out, I substitute dry cannellini beans. The French call this style of dish "en cocotte," "in a Dutch oven." It is served at the table in the cocotte.

SERVES 6

1 pound dry cannellini beans, soaked overnight, or 5 pounds fresh cranberry beans in their pods

2¼ pounds boned leg of lamb, trimmed of all fat, cut into 2-inch pieces, or four 1-pound lamb shanks, each sawed into 3 pieces

¼ cup flour

Salt

Freshly ground black pepper

2 tablespoons olive oil

1 teaspoon ground cumin

2 tablespoons honey

1 cup finely chopped onions

3 large carrots, each cut into 3 pieces crosswise and quartered

2 cups homemade or commercial chicken stock

3 sprigs fresh thyme tied with 4 sprigs parsley and 1 bay leaf

Cover the cannellini beans (after soaking them overnight) with cold water in a large pot. Bring to a boil for 10 minutes. Drain in a colander set in the sink, refresh under cold water, and reserve.

Or shell the fresh cranberry beans and reserve.

Pat the meat dry with paper towels; season the flour with a large pinch of salt and freshly ground pepper.

In a large skillet, heat the oil over medium heat. Dip a few pieces of meat at a time into the flour and place in the skillet. Brown the meat evenly.

Put all the meat back in the skillet with the cooking juices. Sprinkle with salt, freshly ground pepper, and cumin. Drizzle honey over the meat and sauté over medium heat for 2–3 minutes, shaking the pan all the while. Transfer the meat to a 7¼-quart Dutch oven.

In the same skillet, brown the onion and carrots until light golden (about 5 minutes), adding more oil if necessary. Season with salt and freshly ground pepper.

Add the vegetables and the beans to the meat and pour the stock over. Place the herb bouquet on top. Cover tightly. Simmer over medium-low heat for 1½ hours or until the beans are tender, adding salt to the beans about halfway through cooking.

Serve the stew piping hot from the Dutch oven at the table.

note

If this stew is prepared ahead of time, refrigerate the meat and the beans separately. Bring back to room temperature before reheating.

moroccan lamb with prunes and apricots

With this Moroccan stew, I serve couscous as well as with the Tagine of Lamb with Zucchini on page 58.

SERVES
4 TO 6

4 lamb shanks, each sawed into two pieces crosswise, or 4 pounds leg of lamb, not boned, cut into 8 pieces
2 tablespoons olive oil
1 tablespoon ground cumin
$1/8$ teaspoon pulverized saffron or a large pinch of saffron strands
Salt
Freshly ground black pepper
1 cup whole dried California apricots
1 cup whole prunes
2 tablespoons butter
$1/2$ cup chopped onions

In a 4-quart Dutch oven or a pan just large enough to hold the meat, toss the lamb with the oil, cumin, the saffron, salt, and lots of freshly ground pepper—about 15 grinds of the pepper mill.

Pour water over the meat just to cover. Bring slowly to a boil, skimming the foam that rises to the top. Add another $1/2$ cup water. Bring back to a light boil, lower the heat, and partially cover the pot. Simmer for 2 hours or until the meat is fork-tender, turning once in a while.

Meanwhile, soak the apricots and prunes in 2 cups water for 1 hour. Drain, reserving the soaking water.

Twenty minutes before the lamb is ready, melt the butter in a large skillet over medium heat, add the onions and $1/4$ cup water, cover, and simmer for 5 minutes. Raise the heat and add the apricots and prunes. Sauté for 3 minutes and season with salt and freshly ground pepper. Add the reserved soaking liquid, cover, and simmer gently for 15 minutes. Reserve in the skillet.

Transfer the meat to a heated serving bowl and cover with foil. Boil the cooking juices down to less than 1 cup. Reheat the fruits. Pour the reduced sauce over the meat and decorate with the fruits.

Serve with couscous. (See Tagine of Lamb with Zucchini for cooking instructions.)

tagine of lamb with zucchini

A tagine is a North African stew of beef, lamb, or fowl. It takes its name from the clay utensil in which it was originally cooked. I was inspired by Paula Wolfert's recipe for lamb and zucchini in her book *Couscous and Other Good Food from Morocco.* I am always searching for attractive ways to prepare zucchini; for this tagine, I grated the zucchini into long strands.

I serve this tagine over couscous, the North African grain made out of semolina flour. Buy couscous in health food stores or in gourmet shops; avoid the instant couscous found in some supermarkets.

SERVES 6

3 pounds very lean leg of lamb, cut into 2-inch cubes
4 tablespoons butter
1 teaspoon sugar
1 cup sliced onions
1 tablespoon minced garlic
4 sprigs fresh parsley
$1/8$ teaspoon pulverized saffron or a large pinch of saffron strands
$1/2$ teaspoon turmeric
$1/4$ teaspoon crushed red pepper flakes
1 teaspoon dried oregano
2 pounds small zucchini
1 tablespoon salt

For the couscous:
Salt
2 tablespoons olive oil
1 cup couscous, not the quick-cooking kind
Large pinch of saffron strands

Pat the meat dry with paper towels. Melt 3 tablespoons butter over moderate heat in a large skillet and brown the meat evenly, a few pieces at a time, sprinkling sugar over the meat. Adjust the heat to avoid burning the butter. It will take about 20 minutes to brown the lamb evenly. Transfer the meat to a $5^{1}/_{2}$-quart Dutch oven and reserve.

Add the onion, garlic, parsley, and spices to the skillet and cook, stirring with a wooden spoon, for 1 minute. Add to the meat.

Pour 1 cup water into the skillet and bring to a boil while stirring. Add to the meat, cover the pot, and simmer over moderate heat for 2 hours, stirring now and then. Be sure to let the water condensation on the underside of the lid fall back into the pot.

Meanwhile, cut off the ends of the zucchini. Fit the food processor with the largest grater and grate the zucchini into long spaghetti-like strands.

Put the zucchini in a large colander set in the sink and sprinkle 1 tablespoon salt over it. Let sit for 30 minutes. Rinse off the salt and squeeze the zucchini as dry as possible.

In a large skillet, melt the remaining 1 tablespoon butter over medium heat, add the zucchini, and cook for 5 minutes over medium heat or until all the water is evaporated.

Add the zucchini to the lamb and cook for another 15 minutes.

Prepare the couscous: In a small saucepan, season $1/2$ cup water with a large pinch of salt, 1 tablespoon olive oil, and the saffron, and bring to a boil.

In a large bowl, pour the boiling liquid over the couscous, fluff the couscous with the tines of a fork, then rub the couscous with your hands to remove lumps. Set aside for $1/2$ hour.

Using either a couscoussier or an improvised one—a colander set in a stockpot—wrap the couscous in cheesecloth and steam over boiling water for 30 minutes.

Serve the couscous in a bowl, drizzled with 1 tablespoon olive oil and fluffed with the tines of 2 forks, alongside the lamb stew.

If you wish, prepare the stew several hours ahead of time. Refrigerate. Prepare the couscous while you bring the stew back to room temperature.

Reheat the stew slowly on top of the stove for 10–15 minutes and serve piping hot with the couscous.

notes

59

casserole of lamb chops

Cotelettes Champvallon is a famous French dish from the nineteenth century. There are many versions of this lamb recipe, all excellent. I ask the butcher to saw off the rib ends of the chops to make the chops easier to brown.

SERVES 4

3 tablespoons flour
Salt
Freshly ground black pepper
3 tablespoons olive oil
8 very lean lamb chops, rib ends cut 2 inches above the eye and reserved
2 cups thinly sliced onions
1 tablespoon fresh thyme leaves
1½ pounds white California or Yukon Gold potatoes, cut into ⅛-inch slices, washed and dried
1 cup homemade or commercial chicken stock

Preheat the oven to 400 degrees.

On a plate, mix the flour with a large pinch of salt and freshly ground pepper.

Heat 2 tablespoons oil in a large skillet over medium-high heat. Dip the chops and rib ends, a few at a time, in the flour. Brown the chops for 2 minutes on each side, lowering the heat as needed. Transfer to a plate and reserve.

Heat the remaining oil in the skillet over medium-low heat and add the onions and ¼ cup water. Cover and simmer for 10 minutes, checking the onions occasionally.

Line the bottom of an oiled rectangular or oval 3-quart ovenproof casserole with the onions; cover them with the chops and their juices from the plate. Sprinkle with salt, freshly ground pepper, and thyme.

Cover the meat with potatoes, overlapping the slices very tightly. Pour the stock over the potatoes and season with salt and pepper. Grease one side of a piece of parchment paper and cover the top of the potatoes with it to keep the potatoes from drying out while baking.

Bake in the middle of the oven for 1 hour. Turn the broiler to high; discard the parchment paper. Place the dish about 4 inches away from the heating element for several minutes, just enough to turn the potatoes golden and crisp. Serve piping hot.

note : The casserole can be prepared and baked 1 to 2 hours ahead of time. Before broiling it, reheat the dish in a 300-degree oven for 15 minutes.

moussaka

When I have leftover lamb, I grind it and keep it in the freezer until I am ready to make moussaka. My favorite varieties of eggplants are white, Japanese, and the small Italian eggplants.

2 pounds eggplant
1 cup flour
Salt
Freshly ground black pepper
2 cups vegetable oil
3 tablespoons olive oil
4 cups coarsely ground cooked lamb
1 cup finely chopped onion
1 tablespoon minced garlic
1 tablespoon tomato paste
$^2/_3$ cup Tomato Sauce (page 6)
$^1/_4$ teaspoon crushed hot pepper flakes
3 tablespoons Homemade Breadcrumbs (page 13)
$^3/_4$ cup crumbled feta cheese
1 egg, lightly beaten

Discard the stems of the eggplants and cut them lengthwise into $^1/_8$-inch-thick slices. If the eggplants are more than 12 inches long, cut them in half crosswise before slicing them lengthwise.

Line 2 cookie sheets with double layers of paper towels and place next to the stove. On a large plate, mix 1 cup flour with 2 large pinches of salt and freshly ground pepper. To speed up the frying time, pour 1 cup of oil into each of two large skillets. Heat the oil until it reaches 300 degrees. (To check the temperature, drop a piece of bread into the oil. It should sizzle as soon as it hits the fat.) Keep constant heat under the skillets, adjusting it when necessary.

Dip a few eggplant slices at a time in flour and shake off the excess. Lightly deep-fry them on each side, turning them over with tongs. Transfer the eggplant to the prepared cookie sheets. Pat them dry once more with paper towels to get rid of excess oil. Reserve. Discard the oil in the skillets. Wipe out one of them for the next step.

Heat the olive oil in the skillet over medium-high heat. Sauté the ground lamb for 2–3 minutes; stir in the onion, garlic, tomato paste, and sauce. Season with salt, ground pepper, and the hot pepper. Cover and simmer for 10 minutes over medium-low heat, checking once in a while.

Combine the breadcrumbs, cheese, and egg. Mix with the meat. Taste and adjust seasoning.

Layer the bottom of a 3-quart ovenproof dish with $^1/_3$ of the eggplant slices. Spread half of the lamb mixture and overlap $^1/_3$ of the eggplant on top. Add the remaining meat and cover with the last of the eggplant slices. Cover with aluminum foil.

Preheat the oven to 350 degrees.

Bake for 30 minutes or until the casserole is bubbling on top. Serve with fresh pasta.

The moussaka can be prepared ahead of time. Bring back to room temperature when you are ready to bake it.

pork

I find pork from supermarkets tastier than the more expensive cuts sold in butcher shops, perhaps because it has more fat. So I economize and improve the results at the same time—two birds with one stone. The pork cuts used in stews and braises are cheaper than the pork loin popular for more elegant preparations. In different stores in the United States, pork cuts sometimes have different names; a blade cut in one store may be called a shoulder cut or a picnic pork shoulder in another. In any case, pork shoulder is a tasty staple for stews and braises.

Some dishes require pork rind; you may have to order it in advance from your butcher. If you can't find pork rind at all, buy a picnic pork shoulder, remove the rind, and cut it in several pieces. If you have any extra rind, freeze it for another time. Bone the pork shoulder and use the meat for your stew.

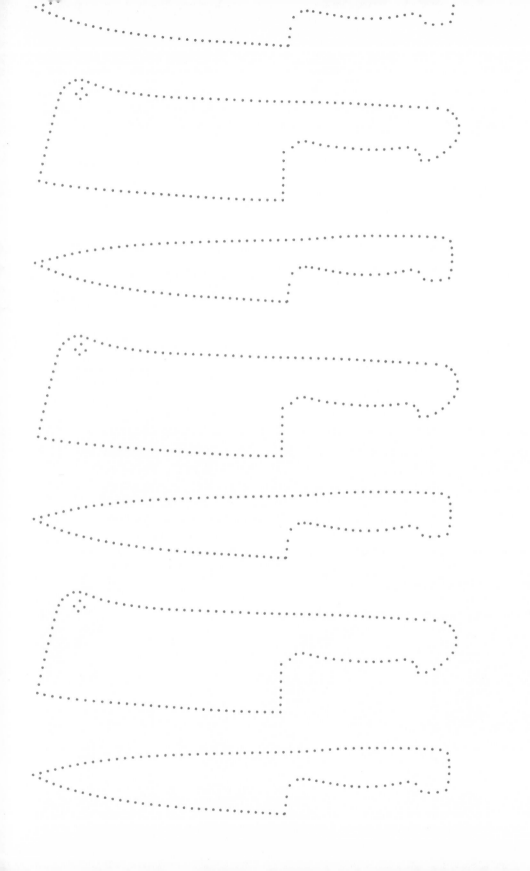

braise of pork roast with onions

In the fall and winter, I prepare this dish at least twice a month for friends who come to dinner unexpectedly. After a quick dash to the supermarket to buy a rib end of pork, onions, and potatoes, I am back in business in no time, cooking a delicious dinner with simple ingredients.

SERVES 4

2 tablespoons olive oil
3 pounds rib-end pork roast with bones, or picnic shoulder
4 cups thinly sliced onions
2 large garlic cloves, peeled and minced
Salt
Freshly ground black pepper
2 sprigs fresh thyme
2 pounds small Yukon Gold potatoes

Heat the oil in a $5\frac{1}{2}$-quart Dutch oven over medium heat and brown the meat on all sides without burning, adjusting the heat accordingly. It will take about 30 minutes to brown the meat evenly. Halfway through the browning process, surround the roast with onions and garlic and stir. When the onions start to color, add 2 tablespoons water to keep them from burning. Season with salt and pepper; add the thyme. Cover the pot and simmer over low heat for $1\frac{1}{2}$ hours, checking the meat once in a while, and letting the steam on the underside of the lid fall back into the pot.

Meanwhile, peel the potatoes and cover them with cold water in a large bowl. Reserve.

After about 1 hour, put the potatoes into the pot and mix them with the onions around the meat for the last 40 minutes of cooking.

Bone the meat the best you can and cut into large chunks. Serve with the potatoes and the onions. Degrease the sauce if necessary. Pass the cooking juices in a sauceboat.

If this braise is prepared ahead of time, reheat slowly for dinner.

note

rolled shoulder of pork braised with winter vegetables

Here is another braised pork dish to serve your family in the long winter months.

SERVES 4

4 tablespoons olive oil
1 14-ounce can plum tomatoes, chopped
2 pounds boned rolled shoulder of pork
Salt
Freshly ground black pepper
1 pound small Yukon Gold potatoes, peeled and quartered
2 medium onions ($\frac{1}{2}$ pound), peeled and quartered
$\frac{1}{2}$ pound small turnips, peeled and quartered
1 pound Granny Smith apples, quartered and cored
6 garlic cloves, unpeeled
4 fresh thyme sprigs

Preheat the oven to 325 degrees.

Drizzle the olive oil in a $7\frac{1}{4}$-quart Dutch oven. Add the chopped tomatoes and their juice. Place the pork on top. Season with salt and freshly ground black pepper.

Cover tightly and bake in the oven for 1 hour.

Meanwhile, in a large bowl, toss together the vegetables, apples, salt, and freshly ground pepper.

After 1 hour of cooking, scatter the vegetables, apples, and garlic around and over the pork. Add thyme on top. Cover and seal the pot, following the instructions on page xv. If you do not seal the pot, be sure to check the pork and add $\frac{1}{4}$ cup water or more to prevent the vegetables from burning. Bake 1 more hour in the oven.

To serve: Break the seal on the pot. Slice the meat on a cutting board and serve it on a heated platter, surrounded by the vegetables.

note

This dish can be prepared several hours ahead of time and slowly reheated on top of the stove.

pork stew with apples and turnips in cider

In the early fall when the apples and small white turnips are at their best, try this simply delicious stew. The tart-sweet apples and the hard cider accent the flavor of pork. Ask the butcher to get pork rind for you.

3 pounds boned pork shoulder, cut into 2-inch cubes
Salt
Freshly ground black pepper
1 tablespoon minced fresh rosemary
4 ounces pork rind
3 tablespoons flour
3 tablespoons olive oil
2$\frac{1}{2}$ cups hard cider
3 cups tart apples, peeled, cored, and cut into eighths
3 cups small white turnips, peeled and cut into eighths
4 garlic cloves, chopped coarsely

**SERVES
4 TO 6**

Place the meat in a mixing bowl and sprinkle with salt, freshly ground pepper, and rosemary. Cover and refrigerate for several hours or overnight.

Roll up the pork rind, tie it with kitchen string, and cover it with cold water in a 2-quart pan. Bring to a light boil and boil for 5 minutes. Drain and cool under cold running water. Set aside.

Pat the meat dry with paper towels.

On a plate, season the flour with a large pinch of salt and freshly ground pepper.

Heat the oil in a large skillet over medium-high heat. Dip a few pieces of pork at a time in the flour, place in the skillet, and brown evenly. As each batch is done, transfer the meat to a 5$\frac{1}{2}$-quart Dutch oven. Pour the cider into the skillet. Over high heat, scrape the bottom of the pan for 1 minute or so to incorporate all the residue. (If the oil and flour in the skillet are burned, skip this step and pour the cider directly into the Dutch oven.)

Strain the cider over the meat; add the apples, turnips, and garlic to the pork; and bury the pork rind in the meat. Season with salt and pepper and cover.

Preheat the oven to 325 degrees.

Seal the pot, following the instructions on page xv. If you do not seal the pot, be sure to check on the pork and add $\frac{1}{4}$ cup of water at a time, if necessary, to prevent the meat or vegetables from burning. Bake in the middle shelf of the oven for 1$\frac{1}{2}$ hours.

Break the seal if you used one. Discard the pork rind, put the stew with the apples and turnips in a heated serving bowl, and skim the fat. Mash some of the apples and turnips into the juices, pour over the meat, and serve immediately.

ragout of curried pork

Pork and curry make a lovely marriage. I choose mild imported Indian curry; hot curry is too spicy for me, but this is up to your taste.

**SERVES
4 TO 6**

3 pounds boned shoulder of pork, cut into 2-inch cubes
1/4 cup flour
Salt
Freshly ground black pepper
3 tablespoons olive oil
2 teaspoons mild curry powder
1/8 teaspoon hot red pepper flakes
1/2 tablespoon minced garlic
1 cup Tomato Sauce (page 6)
1 1/2 cups homemade or commercial chicken stock
1 bouquet garni tied with a string: 3 sprigs fresh thyme, 5 sprigs fresh parsley, 1 bay leaf
2 tablespoons butter
4 medium carrots, peeled and cut into 1-inch slices
1/2 pound small turnips, peeled and quartered
24 pearl onions, peeled
1 tablespoon sugar

Pat the meat dry with paper towels.

On a plate, mix the flour with a large pinch of salt and pepper.

Heat the oil in a 5 1/2-quart Dutch oven over medium-high heat. Dip a few pieces of meat at a time in the flour and brown them evenly on all sides. Transfer the meat back to the Dutch oven and sprinkle with the curry, hot red pepper flakes, salt, and pepper.

Add the garlic and tomato sauce and pour 1 cup of stock over the meat. Place the bouquet garni on top. Cover and simmer for 1 1/2 hours over low heat.

Meanwhile, melt the butter in a 4-quart Dutch oven over medium heat; sauté the vegetables for several minutes, stirring with a wooden spoon; and sprinkle with the sugar, a large pinch of salt, and freshly ground pepper.

Add 1/2 cup chicken stock, cover, and simmer for 20 minutes over low heat.

Add the vegetables and their cooking juices to the pork and cook at a gentle simmer for 30 minutes. Taste and adjust seasoning with salt and pepper.

pork roast braised in beer

In Belgium, beer is a favorite braising liquid for meats and fowl. Here is a tasty dish of braised pork that I ate in a small bistro in Bruges, a lovely Belgian city.

SERVES 4

3 tablespoons lard or oil
3 pounds rib-end pork loin, not boned
8 cups thinly sliced onions
Salt
Freshly ground black pepper
2 cups light beer
3 sprigs fresh thyme
1 bay leaf

Preheat the oven to 325 degrees.

Heat 2 tablespoons lard or oil in a 5^1/$_2$-quart Dutch oven over medium heat. Brown the meat on all sides, turning it over every 5 minutes, and adjusting the heat once in a while. The browning will take about 15 to 20 minutes. Transfer the meat to a plate, sprinkle with salt and freshly ground pepper, and set aside.

Wipe the burned particles out of the bottom of the pot. In the pot, heat the remaining lard or oil over medium heat and stir in the onions, 2 tablespoons water, salt, and pepper. Lower the heat and, stirring frequently, wilt the onions until they start glazing to a honey color, about 20 minutes.

Add the meat with its juice from the plate to the onions. Pour the beer over the meat and onions.

Place the thyme and the bay leaf on top of the meat; cover tightly. Seal the pot, following the instructions on page xv; otherwise, be sure to check on the meat now and then, adding more beer if necessary. Bake for 2 hours in the middle of the oven.

Break the seal on the pot, transfer the meat to a cutting board, cut it into ^{1}/$_4$-inch slices, place on a heated platter, cover, and set aside.

Discard the thyme and bay leaf and reheat the onion sauce on top of the stove, degreasing following the instructions on page xiv.

Ladle the sauce over the meat and serve.

braised spareribs with winter vegetables

My aunt Tatane loved pork spareribs and came up with this succulent concoction. I make it often during the winter. Buy country spareribs, or back ribs that have more meat on them, but be sure there is some fat on them to flavor the vegetables.

SERVES 4

4 pounds country spareribs
3 medium carrots, cut into $1/2$-inch slices
2 cups coarsely chopped onions
1 pound small Yukon Gold potatoes, peeled and quartered
$1/2$ pound small turnips, peeled and quartered
2 large garlic cloves, peeled and chopped
Salt
Freshly ground pepper
1 large sprig fresh thyme
Small bowl of mustard
Small bowl of horseradish

Preheat the broiler to high.

Put the ribs fat side down on the rack of a broiler pan; broil 4 inches from the heating element, turning once, until they are brown and crisp on both sides. With large tongs, transfer the ribs to a platter and reserve.

In a large bowl, combine the vegetables, garlic, salt, and pepper. Add the vegetables to the drippings from the broiler pan (there should be at least 2 tablespoons fat; if not, add oil) with $2/3$ cup water and stir.

Preheat the oven to 350 degrees.

Transfer the vegetables to a $5^1/2$-quart Dutch oven, put the ribs on top of the vegetables, and put the thyme on top. Cover and seal the pot, following the instructions on page xv; otherwise, be sure to check the pork and add $1/4$ cup of water, if necessary, to prevent the meat or vegetables from burning. Bake in the middle of the oven for 2 hours.

Break the seal and serve the pork in the pot, with mustard and horseradish on the side.

pot-au-feu of pork

This pot-au-feu, a specialty of the Perigord in southwestern France, is a favorite of mine for summer buffets and picnics. It has an interesting feature: boiled, the meat does not shrink as it would if braised in a small amount of liquid.

4 pounds boned, rolled shoulder of pork
2 large garlic cloves, cut into 12 slivers
1 teaspoon dried oregano
Salt
Freshly ground black pepper
2 small onions, quartered and stuck with 2 cloves each
4 large carrots, peeled and cut crosswise into 2-inch slices
Bouquet garni: 4 sprigs parsley, 2 sprigs thyme, 1 stalk celery, and 1 bay leaf, tied with kitchen string

SERVES 6

Pat the meat dry with paper towels.

Make small incisions in the meat with the blade of a small knife and bury the garlic in them. Rub oregano, salt, and freshly ground pepper over the meat and put it in a mixing bowl. Cover and refrigerate overnight.

Add cold water to cover the meat in a 5^1/$_2$-quart Dutch oven and bring the water to a boil. Skim the foam that rises to the top. Lower the heat, cover the pot, and simmer for 1 hour.

Uncover, raise the heat a notch, and cook until the water is evaporated, about 1 more hour.

As soon as most of the water has evaporated, discard the bouquet garni.

Lower the heat and turn the meat over to baste with the remaining fat. Transfer meat and vegetables to a platter.

Set aside to cool. Cut the meat into very thin slices and serve on top of the vegetables with the jellied juices. For a picnic, put the sliced meat and vegetables in separate containers.

braised pork chops à la napolitaine

I prefer shoulder pork chops to the center loin—they are juicier.

SERVES 4

3 tablespoons flour
Salt
Freshly ground black pepper
3 tablespoons olive oil
Four ³/₄-inch-thick shoulder pork chops (about 2¹/₂ pounds)
2 cups thinly sliced onions
1 cup white wine, preferably Chardonnay
2 cups Tomato Sauce (page 6)
1¹/₂ pounds Yukon Gold potatoes, peeled and sliced ¹/₈ inch thick, washed and dried

On a plate, season the flour with salt and pepper.

Heat the oil in a large skillet over medium heat. Dip the chops in the flour, shake off excess, and brown 2 chops at a time for several minutes on each side. Transfer them to an oiled 3-quart rectangular ovenproof baking dish. Season with salt and freshly ground pepper.

Put the onions with 2 tablespoons water into the same skillet, lower the heat, and, stirring with a wooden spoon, cook until barely wilted. Cover the chops with the onions.

Add 1 cup white wine to the skillet, raise the heat, and bring to a boil, scraping the bottom of the pan to incorporate the drippings. Reserve.

Preheat oven to 325 degrees.

Ladle the tomato sauce over the onions and chops.

Place the potatoes on top of the tomato sauce in one layer, overlapping tightly. Season with salt and pepper and add the reserved wine.

Cover the potatoes with buttered parchment paper and bake for 1 hour.

To serve, set the broiler on high, uncover the dish, and broil 6 inches from the heating element for about 3–4 minutes until the potatoes are just colored.

note Prepare the dish up to the broiler step 1 to 2 hours ahead of time if you wish. Then reheat for 10 minutes or so in a 300-degree oven before broiling.

rougaille of sausages

Rougaille is a Madagascar Creole word meaning stew. The dish originated in the French-speaking islands of the Indian Ocean, where the food has been influenced by the African, French, and Chinese people who came to live there and blended their various cuisines. Rougaille can be made with all kinds of meat or fish.

4 tablespoons olive oil

2 cups finely chopped onions

3 cups peeled, seeded, and finely chopped fresh tomatoes

1½ tablespoons tomato paste

1 tablespoon minced ginger

1 tablespoon minced garlic

Salt

2 tablespoons turmeric

1 teaspoon hot pepper flakes, or 1 jalapeño pepper, chopped

2 bay leaves

2 sprigs fresh thyme

½ pound slab bacon or pancetta

2 pounds sweet pork sausages (or a mixture of sweet and smoked), cut into 3-inch pieces

SERVES 4

In a 5½-quart Dutch oven, heat 3 tablespoons olive oil over medium-high heat. Stir in the onions, add ¼ cup water, and cook uncovered for 10 minutes, watching that they do not burn.

Stir the tomatoes, tomato paste, ginger, and garlic into the onions. Sprinkle with salt, turmeric, and red pepper flakes (or the jalapeño pepper) and stir. Add the bay leaves and thyme, cover, and simmer for 20 minutes over medium-low heat.

Meanwhile, in a 2-quart pan, cover the bacon with cold water and bring to a gentle boil for 5 minutes. Drain the bacon and cut it into ½-inch cubes.

With the tines of a fork, prick the sausages all over to prevent them from bursting while cooking.

In a large skillet, heat 1 tablespoon oil over medium heat, and brown the bacon and the sausages together for 10 minutes. Stir the meat into the onion-tomato stew, cover, and simmer for 1½ hours over low heat.

The stew gains in flavor when made 2 or 3 days ahead of time.

note

cassoulet

This is a great dish for a party but it needs good planning.

I make cassoulet once a year and I consider my production like vintage wines—some years are better than others.

There are many versions of cassoulet, the most famous ones are from Castelnaudary, Toulouse, and Bordeaux, large cities in southwestern France.

I make mine the Toulouse way, with lamb in addition to pork and duck confit. For me, the beans are the most important part of the cassoulet; they should not get mushy and should be very tasty. I cook the beans in a rich homemade chicken stock with pork rind and sausages. The rind binds the juices together, making the beans taste rich and smooth.

I make my own duck confit but you can buy good commercial confit and goose fat. I cook the lamb stew 2 or 3 days before I start on the beans.

**SERVES 10
OR MORE**

Duck Confit (page 108) or commercial confit
Spring Lamb Stew (page 53)

For the beans:
2 pounds dried cannellini or great Northern beans
8 tablespoons goose fat
1 cup thinly sliced onion
4 tablespoons minced garlic
1 28-ounce can Italian plum tomatoes, coarsely chopped
Salt
$1/8$ teaspoon red pepper flakes
3 ounces pork rind, rolled and tied with string
$1/2$ pound slab bacon or pancetta
1 pound garlicky pork sausage
3 sprigs fresh thyme
3 quarts Rich Chicken Stock (page 7)
$1/4$ cup minced parsley
1 cup coarse Homemade Breadcrumbs (page 13)

Soak the beans overnight in a large quantity of water in a 9-quart Dutch oven or in 2 smaller pots.

The next day, bring the beans and water to a rolling boil. Drain the beans in a colander set in the kitchen sink. Refresh under cold running water and pick out and discard all the shriveled beans. Set aside.

Melt 4 tablespoons goose fat in the 9-quart Dutch oven or in 2 smaller pots over medium heat. Add the onions and stir occasionally until the onions are translucent.

Add 1 tablespoon minced garlic and the chopped tomatoes with their juice; sprinkle with salt and red pepper flakes. Cover and cook for 10 minutes, stirring occasionally.

Meanwhile, cover the pork rind and slab bacon or pancetta with cold water in a 3-quart pan and bring to a boil for 5 minutes. Drain and refresh under cold water and set aside.

Add the beans to the tomato and onion mixture, and bury the pork rind, the pancetta, the sausage, and the fresh thyme in the beans. *Do not salt yet.* Pour 2 quarts chicken broth over the beans and meat. Cover tightly and simmer over medium heat for 1½ hours. After 30 minutes of cooking, remove the sausages and reserve for the final assembly of the cassoulet. Season the beans with salt and simmer for another hour over low to medium heat or until tender.

The cassoulet can be prepared ahead of time; reserve beans and cooking liquid separately (otherwise the beans would keep swelling and get mushy). Reserve the bacon or pancetta, pork rind, and sausages together and cover.

The morning of the day you plan to serve the cassoulet, reheat the duck confit to melt the fat, following the instructions on page 108.

Preheat the oven to 325 degrees 2 hours before serving.

To assemble the cassoulet: Reheat the beans, their cooking liquid, and the lamb stew in its own cooking juices in a large ovenproof pot. (I use my large 9-quart Dutch oven or 2 smaller pots.)

Cut the bacon or pancetta into small chunks and add them to the beans.

Untie the pork rind, bury it with the duck confit in the beans, and add the minced parsley and garlic (reserving 1 tablespoon of each for later) into the beans, mixing well.

Taste the beans and add more salt if necessary.

Cut the reserved sausage into ¼-inch slices and place on top of the beans.

Sprinkle with the breadcrumbs and remaining parsley and garlic. Drizzle 4 tablespoons melted goose fat over the top.

Bake for 1 hour or until the top browns and bubbles. Once in a while, break up the crust and add more chicken broth to keep the beans moist.

Just before serving, reheat about 2–3 cups chicken stock.

Serve piping hot with hot chicken broth in a sauceboat to ladle over the individual portions of cassoulet.

baeckhofe

Baeckhofe "baked in the baker's oven" is an Alsatian specialty. It is a superb dish, very easy to prepare, and one of my very favorites for a large family dinner. Alsace is a province dividing France from Germany with the Rhine River as the boundary. Years ago, in Alsatian villages, the baeckhofe was baked in the dying heat of the baker's oven after the bread was ready for midday dinner. A pot was specially made for this dish, something like a crockpot with a tight-fitting lid sealed with a flour paste.

Alsace is famous for its goose products, and goose fat is prized. You should be able to find goose fat in specialty stores or delicatessens; it freezes very well. If you cannot find any, use rendered chicken fat.

SERVES 8

2 pounds boned pork shoulder, cut into 2-inch pieces
2 pounds boned leg of lamb, cut into 2-inch pieces
1/4 pound pork rind, cut into 2-inch pieces

For the marinade:
1 large garlic clove, peeled
1 medium onion, peeled and quartered
Salt
Freshly ground black pepper
1 bottle (750 ml) of white wine, Alsatian or Chardonnay
1 large sprig fresh thyme
1 bay leaf

For the vegetables:
4 cups finely chopped onions
4 cups finely chopped leek whites
8 cups Yukon Gold potatoes, peeled and cut into 1/4-inch slices
6 tablespoons goose fat or rendered chicken fat

In a mixing bowl just large enough, combine meats, garlic, and quartered onion. Season with salt and freshly ground pepper and pour the wine over the meat. Add thyme and bay leaf and cover. Refrigerate overnight.

Strain the mixture in a colander set over a large mixing bowl. Reserve the meats and liquid separately.

In a large mixing bowl, mix potatoes, chopped onions, and leeks. Season with salt and freshly ground pepper and mix once more thoroughly. Make 2 piles of the vegetable mixture.

Preheat the oven to 325 degrees.

Grease a 7$\frac{1}{4}$-quart Dutch oven with 2 tablespoons goose fat. Add half of the vegetable mixture; spread the meats on top with 2 more tablespoons goose fat; cover the meat with the remaining vegetables and goose fat. Add the reserved liquid and cover tightly. Seal the pot, following the instructions on page xv; otherwise, be sure to check on the meats now and again. Add about $\frac{1}{4}$ cup water at a time if the meat and vegetables are drying out.

Bake in the oven for 3 hours. Turn off the oven but leave the pot in it for another $\frac{1}{2}$ hour.

Break the seal at the table, uncover, and before serving, inhale the delicious aroma that emanates from the pot.

choucroute garnie

A choucroute is a dish of sauerkraut braised in white wine with a garnish of bacon, both fresh and smoked sausages, and boiled potatoes. Sauerkraut is shredded cabbage marinated in salt brine. In the States, sauerkraut has been maligned and is indeed often tasteless, overcooked, and soggy. Cooked and seasoned properly, however, it is a delicious vegetable, slightly acidic and crunchy. The best sauerkraut is the kind sold in wooden barrels in delicatessens; if that is not available, try the sauerkraut sold in plastic bags.

I choose a mellow white wine for the braising liquids, and I add sugar to offset the high acid content of the sauerkraut. Geese are raised commercially in Alsace for pâtés and confits, and goose fat is used for all Alsatian traditional dishes. Goose fat is easily available in the States, through catalogs or in butcher shops.

SERVES 6

3 pounds sauerkraut
1 pound Canadian bacon, in one piece
1 pound bacon, sliced into 1/4-inch-thick pieces
6 knockwurst
1 large kielbasa
7 tablespoons goose fat
2 1/2 cups finely chopped onions
3 garlic cloves, coarsely chopped
2 Granny Smith apples, peeled and cut into small cubes
12 juniper berries
Salt
1 teaspoon sugar
1 sprig of thyme, 1 bay leaf, 1 clove, and several crushed peppercorns wrapped in cheesecloth
1 bottle white wine, Riesling or Chardonnay
6 medium-size Yukon Gold potatoes, peeled
6 frankfurters
Mustard
Horseradish

Wash the sauerkraut several times in lots of cold water. Cover it with cold water in a large stockpot and bring to a rolling boil. Quickly drain it in a colander set in the sink and cool it under cold running water for 1 minute. Reserve in the colander.

Cover the Canadian bacon, bacon slices, knockwurst, and kielbasa (but not the frankfurters) with a large amount of cold water in a large kettle. Bring to a boil, cover, lower the heat, and simmer for 20 minutes. Reserve 1 cup of cooking liquid. Drain the meats and reserve for later.

Preheat the oven to 325 degrees.

In a 7$\frac{1}{4}$-quart Dutch oven, melt the goose fat over medium heat, add the onions and garlic, and stir with a wooden spoon for 2–3 minutes, coating the onions with the fat.

Stir in the sauerkraut, apples, and juniper berries. Season with salt and 1 teaspoon sugar. Bury the spices wrapped in cheesecloth and add the wine. Cover tightly and braise in the middle of the oven for half an hour.

Add the reserved cooked sausages and bacons, adding a small amount of the reserved sausage liquid if the sauerkraut seems to dry out (it should be juicy but not swimming in liquid). Braise for another 30 minutes. The choucroute can be prepared ahead of time to this step.

Reheat the sauerkraut very slowly on top of the stove. Meanwhile, in a large saucepan, cover the potatoes with cold salted water. Bring to a boil, partially covered, and cook for 20 minutes or until tender. Drain right away and keep warm in a heated bowl.

Prick the frankfurters all over with a fork and cover them with a large amount of water; bring to a light boil and simmer for 15 minutes. Drain the frankfurters and add them to the potatoes.

With tongs, remove the Canadian bacon and cut it into thick slices. Transfer the sauerkraut to a large heated platter and decorate with all the sausages and the boiled potatoes. Serve with the mustard and horseradish on the side.

stuffed cabbage lasagna

When I have leftover meat from a stew, I grind it and freeze it. With ground lamb, I prepare Moussaka, a Greek dish with eggplant (page 61). With ground pork, I make a pork and cabbage lasagna: layers of ground meat and cabbage leaves with a white sauce on top. Because the pork is already cooked, this is a relatively quick dish to prepare.

SERVES 8

3 pounds savoy cabbage
1 tablespoon olive oil
1 pound leftover cooked pork, ground
1 cup finely chopped onion
1 tablespoon minced garlic
1 tablespoon tomato paste
$^2/_3$ cup Tomato Sauce (page 6)
Salt
Freshly ground black pepper
$^1/_4$ teaspoon crushed hot pepper flakes
$^1/_2$ cup grated Parmesan or Gruyère cheese
1 egg, lightly beaten
2 cups White Sauce (page 5)

Discard the tough outer cabbage leaves. Gently separate the remaining leaves from the stalk, using a small pointed knife to help disengage the leaves.

Bring 6 quarts of salted water to a boil in a stockpot, add the cabbage leaves, and bring back to a boil for 10 minutes or until the leaves are semisoft.

Drain the cabbage in a colander set in the kitchen sink to cool.

Heat the oil in a large nonstick skillet over medium heat and brown the ground meat for 2 minutes; add the onion, garlic, tomato paste, and tomato sauce and stir. Sprinkle with salt, freshly ground pepper, and hot pepper flakes. Cover and cook over low to medium heat for 10 minutes, checking to be sure that nothing burns.

Set aside 2 tablespoons of grated cheese. With a wooden spoon, whisk the egg into the ground meat with the remaining cheese.

Preheat the oven to 400 degrees.

Make three piles of cabbage leaves. Layer 1/3 of the cabbage leaves in a buttered 3-quart rectangular or oval ovenproof baking dish. Sprinkle with salt and spread half the ground meat over the cabbage. Layer more cabbage leaves over the stuffing and add the remaining meat stuffing. Cover with the last of the cabbage leaves.

Pour the white sauce over the cabbage and sprinkle with the reserved cheese. Cover the dish with parchment paper.

Bake the casserole in the middle of the oven for 15 minutes; discard the parchment, and continue cooking until the cheese browns slightly. Serve piping hot.

This dish can be prepared several hours ahead of time before being baked in the oven.

note

83

poultry
& game

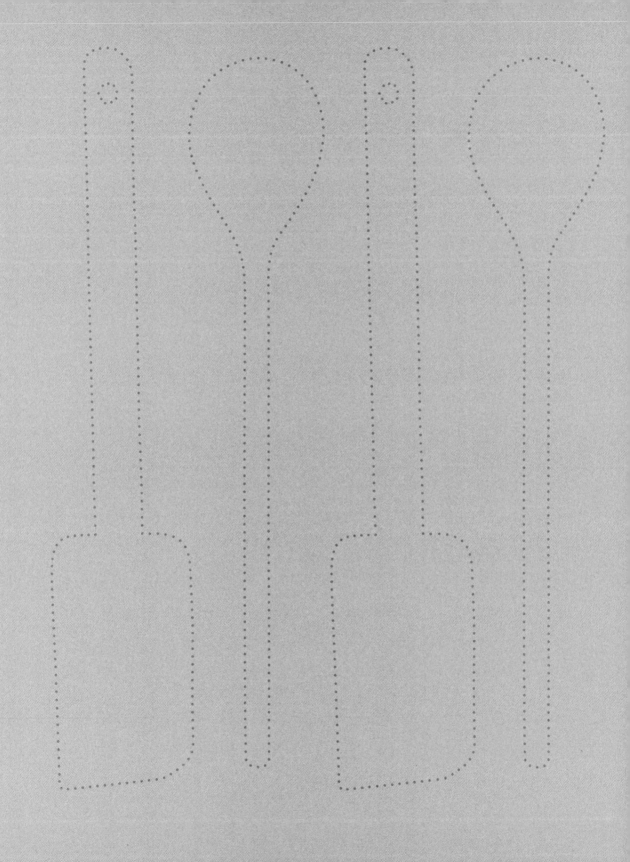

King Henry IV of Navarre, in the sixteenth century, wanted all his citizens to have a poule au pot (a braised chicken) at least once a week; today, chicken is common in our daily fare.

I always buy whole chickens and ducks. To save time, I ask the butcher to cut them up for me and to chop the carcass into several pieces. When I cook duck or chicken, I use the carcass to add flavor, or I keep it for a stock. I don't keep many foods frozen, but duck and chicken carcasses freeze nicely.

I also trim fat off the chicken or duck and render it for cooking; it's economical and delicious.

When you are making a rabbit dish, always try to get a fresh-killed rabbit; frozen rabbit can be dry. You may have to order fresh rabbit in advance.

chicken à la grecque

Years ago, in New York, I would cross Eighth Avenue from my house to La Bonbonnière, our friendly Greek diner, where I ate breakfast, drinking coffee with Lou and Zoé Condax, the owners, who held forth behind the counter. The "early birds" consisted of my husband, called the "professor" (he read the *New York Times*), Louie the gasket specialist, Sal from the auto-body shop, and a dump-truck operator known as Pork Chop. Then came later arrivals, the "cab-hailing types" who went to work uptown and invariably talked about food and swapped recipes; Lou's chicken recipe from Poulithra was a winner and a great favorite in my family. After Lou and Zoé sold the diner to go back to Greece, I never crossed the avenue again for breakfast; an era had ended, but Lou's chicken still figures in my menus today.

SERVES 4

One 3-pound chicken
2 tablespoons olive oil
1½ cups diced onions
1 tablespoon minced garlic
Salt
Freshly ground black pepper
2 cups Tomato Sauce (page 6)
6 ounces feta cheese, grated

Ask the butcher to cut the chicken into legs, thighs, breast, and wings. Freeze the carcass for a stock.
    Trim and discard all the fat around the chicken pieces.
    In a large skillet, heat 2 tablespoons oil over moderate heat and brown the chicken evenly, a few pieces at a time, starting with the skin side down. The browning will take about 20 minutes. Transfer the chicken pieces to a plate and set aside.
    Reserve 2 tablespoons of fat in the skillet (or add more oil if necessary), and add the onions, garlic, and ¼ cup water. Sprinkle with salt and pepper, cover, and simmer over low to medium heat for 15 minutes, occasionally checking to be sure that the onions are wilting and not burning.
    Preheat oven to 350 degrees.
    Layer the onions and garlic in an oiled deep 3-quart ovenproof dish, cover with tomato sauce, and place the chicken pieces on top with the juices from the plate. Sprinkle with salt and pepper, and cover with foil or greased parchment paper.
    Cook for 40 minutes in the middle of the oven. Uncover and sprinkle with the grated feta cheese. Bake for another 15 minutes or until the cheese melts over the chicken.
Serve immediately.

country captain

This is an Indian chicken curry, a favorite dish in America in the first half of the twentieth century. Cecily Brownstone, a friend of many years, did research on the name Country Captain. She found the following explanation in *Miss Leslie's New Cookery Book*, published in 1857. "This is an East India dish," wrote Miss Leslie; "the term country captain signifies a captain of the native troops (or Sepoys) in the pay of England. Probably this dish was first introduced to English tables by a Sepoy officer."

SERVES 4

One 3-pound chicken
¼ cup flour
Salt
Freshly ground black pepper
4 tablespoons butter
⅓ cup finely diced onion
⅓ cup seeded and finely diced green pepper
1 garlic clove, peeled and crushed
1 teaspoon hot curry powder or 1½ teaspoons mild curry powder
1 sprig fresh thyme or ½ teaspoon dried thyme
One 14-ounce can Italian plum tomatoes, chopped
3 tablespoons dried currants or raisins, washed and drained
1 cup toasted blanched almonds

Ask the butcher to cut the chicken into pieces: drumsticks, thighs, breast, wings, and the carcass in several pieces.

Trim and discard all the fat around the chicken pieces.

Mix the flour with a large pinch of salt and pepper on a large dish and coat the chicken pieces with the mixture.

Melt the butter in a 5½-quart Dutch oven on moderate heat, avoiding burning the butter. Brown the chicken breast first, skin side down. Turn and brown the other side. Transfer to a plate and continue browning the dark meat and carcass until golden brown. Reserve with the breast. Season with salt and pepper.

Reserve 1 tablespoon of the fat in the pan. Add the onion, green pepper, garlic, curry powder, and thyme to the pot. Stir over low heat and cook for 5 minutes; add the chopped tomatoes with their juice. Season with salt and pepper. Cover and cook over medium heat for 10 minutes.

Add the chicken, skin side up with the juices in the plate. Cover and simmer slowly for 40 minutes. Now and then, uncover and let the condensation on the underside of the lid fall back into the chicken.

Uncover the pot, transfer the chicken pieces to a heated platter, and discard the carcass. Stir the currants or raisins into the sauce and pour the sauce over the chicken. Serve accompanied by the roasted almonds in a small serving bowl to sprinkle on individual portions.

chicken à la cubana

When I was invited to my Cuban friend's house for dinner, I always asked for either this dish, Picadillo (page 32), or Beef Stew à l'Espagnole (page 25), all delicious stews.

SERVES 4

4 chicken legs and thighs (about 3 pounds)
$1/3$ cup golden raisins
2 tablespoons olive oil
Salt
Freshly ground black pepper
$1/2$ cup chopped onion
4 garlic cloves, peeled and smashed
2 tablespoons tomato puree
$2/3$ cup red wine, Zinfandel, Rioja, or Côtes-du-Rhône
2 tablespoons capers, drained
$2/3$ cup green olives with pimentos
1 teaspoon dried thyme or 1 sprig fresh thyme
1 teaspoon ground cumin

Ask the butcher to separate the legs from the thighs and chop off the ends of the legs (freeze the ends for stock). Trim off and discard the fat around the thighs and legs.

Soak the raisins in $1/2$ cup warm water for half an hour.

In a $5^1/2$-quart Dutch oven, heat the oil over medium-low heat. Brown a few chicken pieces at a time (do not crowd the pan), skin side down first. It will take about 15 to 20 minutes to brown all the chicken pieces. Transfer to a plate; season with salt and pepper and reserve.

Reserve 2 tablespoons of the fat in the pot (or add more oil, if necessary). Add the onion and the garlic with 2 tablespoons water; cover and simmer for 5 minutes over low heat.

In a small mixing bowl, whisk the tomato puree into the wine; then pour it over the onions. Add to the pot the capers, olives, drained raisins, and chicken, skin side up, with the juices in the plate. Sprinkle with thyme, cumin, and more salt and pepper.

Cover and braise over medium-low heat for 40 minutes or until tender. Now and then uncover and let the water condensation on the underside of the lid fall into the pot.

chicken à la créole

The Creoles of the Indian Ocean islands, Madagascar and La Réunion, love Chinese spices and cook many dishes with them. Rougaille of Sausages (page 75) is another of their creations. Spicy Ratatouille with Fresh Mint (page 158) is a good accompaniment for this chicken.

SERVES 6

6 chicken legs and thighs (3½ pounds)
3 tablespoons olive oil
Salt
Freshly ground pepper
1½ cups finely chopped onions
1 tablespoon minced garlic
¼ cup minced ginger
1 28-ounce can Italian plum tomatoes, chopped
2½ cups homemade or commercial chicken stock
¼ teaspoon saffron strands
2 tablespoons butter
1½ cups long-grain rice

Ask the butcher to separate the legs from the thighs and to chop 1 inch off the ends of the legs (freeze these for a stock). Trim and discard the fat around the chicken pieces.

Heat 1 tablespoon of the oil in a large skillet over medium-high heat and brown the chicken skin side down first. Browning will take about 20 minutes. Transfer the chicken, skin side up, to a plate. Season with salt and freshly ground pepper and reserve for later.

Meanwhile, heat 2 tablespoons oil in a 5½-quart Dutch oven over medium heat. Add the onions, garlic, and ginger and 2 tablespoons water to the Dutch oven. Cover and cook for 5 minutes.

Add the tomatoes and their juice to the onions. Season with salt and freshly ground pepper. Cook partially covered for 20 minutes, or until the sauce thickens into the consistency of a relish. Stir the sauce once in a while.

Put the chicken pieces skin side up on top of the tomatoes. Pour over the collected juices.

Bring the chicken broth, saffron, a large pinch of salt and butter to a boil and pour it over the rice.

Add the rice to the tomatoes and chicken, cover tightly, and simmer gently for 30 minutes or until the rice is tender. Serve from the casserole.

chicken braised in soy sauce

This is a specialty of Madagascar, the French island off the eastern coast of South Africa.

4 chicken legs and thighs (about 3 pounds)
2 tablespoons olive oil
Salt
Freshly ground pepper
1½ cups finely chopped onions
2 tablespoons grated fresh ginger
2 tablespoons minced garlic
4 tablespoons soy sauce

Ask the butcher to separate the legs from the thighs, chop the thighs into 3 pieces each, chop off the end of the legs (to freeze for a stock), and chop the legs into 2 pieces each. Trim all the fat around the chicken pieces.

In a large skillet, heat the oil over medium heat and brown the chicken, a few pieces at a time. This will take about 20–25 minutes. Transfer the chicken, skin side up, to a 4-quart Dutch oven and season with salt and pepper.

Reserve 2 tablespoons chicken fat in the skillet (or add more oil, if necessary). Over medium heat, add the onions, 2 tablespoons water, ginger, and garlic, and stir for 2–3 minutes.

Add the onion-ginger mixture and the soy sauce to the chicken and mix well.

Cover the pot and braise the chicken over low to medium heat for 40 minutes or until tender. Now and then, uncover the pot and let the water condensation under the lid fall back in the pot. Serve immediately.

chicken fricassée à la célestine

Once upon a time, Madame Célestine Blanchard, a thirty-five-year-old widow, owned a restaurant in the French town of Lyon, where she was famous for her delicious food, yes, but mostly for her great beauty. Her chef fell in love with her; too shy to talk, he poured his love into his cooking and created this simple dish of chicken and tomatoes, calling it Chicken Célestine. When Célestine took her first bite, she fell in love. They were married and lived happily ever after.

You don't need to fall in love at first bite to appreciate this simple dish.

SERVES 2

2 chicken legs and thighs (about 1½ pounds)
2 tablespoons olive oil
Salt
Freshly ground pepper
1 cup Tomato Sauce (page 6)
½ cup heavy cream

Ask the butcher to separate the chicken legs from the thighs and chop off the ends of the legs (freeze these for a stock). Trim and discard the fat around the chicken pieces. Heat the oil in a 4-quart Dutch oven over medium heat. Brown the chicken pieces on all sides, starting skin side down; transfer to a plate. Season with salt and pepper. Set aside.

Discard most of the fat in the pot, raise the heat, and add the tomato sauce and cream. Bring to a light boil while stirring.

Add the chicken pieces skin side up.

Cover tightly and simmer over low to medium heat for 40 minutes or until tender. Now and then, uncover the pot and let the water condensation under the lid fall back into the pot.

Transfer the chicken to a heated platter. Skim off the fat on top of the sauce and ladle the sauce over the chicken.

chicken with forty cloves of garlic

This is a simpler version of the famous Provençal recipe Poulet aux Quarante Gousses d'Ail. Do not be afraid of the large amount of garlic; it mellows while braising. First the garlic is lightly roasted before it is added to the chicken. I make this dish when the first crop of garlic arrives, in June and July.

One 3-pound chicken
2 tablespoons olive oil
Salt
Freshly ground black pepper
3 to 4 heads of garlic, separated into cloves, not peeled
1 cup white wine, preferably Chardonnay
7 fresh or dried bay leaves

SERVES 4

Have the butcher cut the chicken into legs, thighs, breast, and wings, and chop the carcass into several pieces. Trim and discard the fat around the chicken pieces.

In a 5¹/₂-quart Dutch oven, heat the oil over medium heat; add the garlic cloves, and stir them constantly with a wooden spoon for about 5 minutes or until they take on a light golden color. Transfer them to a large plate.

Brown a few pieces of chicken at a time, including the carcass pieces, skin side first. Transfer the chicken to the plate with the garlic and season with salt and pepper.

Reserve 2 tablespoons of fat in the pot (add more oil if necessary). Whisk in the white wine and bring it to a light boil. Add the chicken, skin side up, along with its juices from the plate, and the garlic cloves. Add the bay leaves.

Cover tightly and simmer over medium-low heat for 45 minutes or until the chicken is tender. Now and then, uncover the pot and let the water condensation on the underside of the lid fall back into the pot.

Transfer the chicken and the garlic cloves to a heated platter, discarding the carcass pieces. Decorate with the bay leaves, cover with foil, and set aside. Degrease the pan juices if necessary. Serve the juices in a sauceboat on the side. The peeled garlic is delicious spread on bread.

coq au vin

Years ago I always cooked coq au vin for my husband's birthday; every summer I reserved a year-old rooster for it from our local farm. The roosters were very scrawny once their feathers were removed. I had a hard time cutting them in pieces; the bones and muscles were very tough from all the exercise the roosters had had. But those tough muscles released delicious flavors during the long slow simmer; it was worth all the trouble. I had so many friends who wanted to eat my coq au vin that I usually was left with only the cock's comb to eat, but that was delicious too. Alas, one year I went to get my rooster, and instead of a scrawny thing, the farmer proudly gave me a plump bird. I knew at once that he had fallen into the modern habit of overfeeding his birds. I was so disgusted that I didn't make coq au vin for several years. But one year, I tried it again, this time with a chicken. I had to devise a way to give lots of flavor to the sauce. I knew I could not cook the chicken for several hours as I did with my scrawny rooster. I decided to cook the chicken in less than 1 hour to keep the meat from falling apart, followed by a reduction of the sauce over a gentle boil, degreasing it now and then until it became syrupy and shiny. I flambéed red wine to eliminate the alcohol, and I made a rich chicken stock to compensate for the short cooking time. It worked. Coq au vin is back on my menu.

SERVES 6

One 3-pound chicken plus 2 thighs and 2 legs
2 1/2 cups red wine, Côtes-du-Rhône or Zinfandel
1 1/2 tablespoons tomato paste
2 tablespoons olive oil
Salt
Freshly ground black pepper
3 tablespoons flour
2 cups Rich Chicken Stock (page 7)
3 sprigs fresh thyme
1 bay leaf

For the garnish:
1/4 pound pearl onions
1/4 pound slab bacon or pancetta
1/2 tablespoon olive or vegetable oil
1/2 pound small white mushrooms (stems discarded), cut into wedges

Ask the butcher to cut the chicken into several pieces: drumsticks, thighs, wings, chicken breast, and the carcass in several pieces. Trim and discard all the fat around each piece of chicken.

In a large skillet, bring the wine to a rolling boil (it will not flambé otherwise). Strike a match into the wine, keeping your face away from the skillet. The wine should light up quickly with spectacular 5-inch-high flames (if it doesn't, just boil the wine for 2 minutes). Gently shake the skillet handle until the flames die out, about 2 minutes. Mix in the tomato paste and reserve for later in a small mixing bowl.

Pat the skillet dry and heat 2 tablespoons oil over medium heat. Brown a few pieces of chicken at a time, including the carcass pieces, skin side down first over medium heat, adding more oil if necessary. Transfer all the chicken but the breast to a 7½-quart Dutch oven. Sprinkle with salt and pepper and reserve. Set aside the chicken breast for later.

Reserve 3 tablespoons fat in the skillet or add more oil if necessary. Over moderate heat, whisk the fat with 3 tablespoons flour until the mixture is smooth. Switch to a wooden spoon and stir the mixture constantly until it turns the color of hazelnut, adjusting the heat. This will take about 5 minutes.

Whisk the wine into the skillet and bring to a boil; it will thicken in 1 or 2 minutes; whisk in the stock and bring once more to a boil. Strain the sauce over the chicken in the Dutch oven.

Add the thyme and bay leaf. Cover with a piece of greased parchment paper and the lid.

Bring the chicken to a boil. Immediately lower the heat and simmer gently for 50 minutes.

Add the reserved chicken breasts. Cover and cook over medium heat for 5 more minutes. Transfer the chicken to a heated platter, discarding the carcass pieces. Cover with foil and reserve in a warm place.

Degrease the sauce, following the instructions on page xiv (it will need degreasing); the sauce will take about 15 minutes to get syrupy and shiny.

Meanwhile, prepare the garnish: Cover the pearl onions with cold water in a pan and bring to a boil for 2 minutes or so. Drain and refresh under cold water. Peel the onions and reserve.

Cut off the excess fat on the bacon. Cut the bacon into ¼-inch slices, then cut each slice crosswise into ½-inch pieces (called lardons).

Heat ½ tablespoon oil in a large skillet and brown the bacon or pancetta with the onions until the onions are lightly golden. Transfer to a plate and set aside.

Add more fat to the skillet if necessary and sauté the mushrooms for 2 minutes. Sprinkle with salt and freshly ground pepper. Cover and cook for another 5 minutes.

Decorate the chicken with the garnish, ladle some sauce over it, and serve the remaining sauce in a sauceboat. Steamed potatoes sprinkled with minced parsley are the classic accompaniment.

chicken potpie

My aunt Tatane cooked for one of the great French actors of the 1930s, Harry Baur, who played Jean Valjean in the first movie of *Les Misérables*. Baur was a fine gourmet and gourmand and loved my aunt's cooking. Once, from England, where he was shooting the film *Volpone*, he brought back a recipe for chicken potpie. He must have given the recipe orally to Tatane, who wrote it down in her cooking notebook as *Chiquen Paille*, which roughly translates as "chicken straw."

The dish is not difficult to make, but it takes time to prepare because it has so many ingredients. Remember that all the preparation can be done ahead of time. If you are not a pastry maker, just cover the dish, and it will still be delicious without the pastry.

SERVES 6

One 3-pound chicken, plus 1 chicken thigh and 1 chicken leg
2 tablespoons butter
1 tablespoon olive oil
Salt
Freshly ground black pepper
2 cups sliced onions
2 medium carrots, peeled and sliced thin
$1/2$ pound small white mushrooms or chanterelles, stems removed, quartered
1 teaspoon minced garlic
1 pound sweet Italian pork sausages, sliced into 1-inch pieces
2 tablespoons flour
1 veal kidney, cut into 2-inch cubes, all gristle and fat removed
1 cup heavy cream or light cream
2 sprigs fresh tarragon
3 hard-boiled eggs, each quartered
$1/2$ cup green picholine olives
1 sprig fresh thyme
Pastry Dough for Potpies (page 10)
1 egg yolk mixed with 1 tablespoon water for glazing the pastry

Ask the butcher to cut the chicken into legs (with the ends chopped off), thighs, the breast in 4 pieces, and the carcass in several pieces. (Freeze the carcass and the ends of the legs for stock.)

In a large skillet, heat the butter and oil slowly. Brown the breast pieces first, skin side down, over moderate heat. Transfer them to a large plate.

Brown a few chicken pieces at a time, over moderate heat, without burning the fat in the skillet (about 20 minutes). Brown the carcass pieces to add flavor to the cooking juices.

Transfer the chicken pieces and carcass to the plate with the breasts. Season with salt and freshly ground pepper. Reserve.

Reserve 2 tablespoons of fat in the skillet (or add more oil, if necessary), and add the onions and carrots with 2 tablespoons water. Season with a large pinch of salt and freshly ground pepper. Cook over moderate heat for 10 minutes, stirring once in a while. Transfer the onions and carrots to a deep round 3-quart ovenproof dish.

In the same skillet, sauté the mushrooms and garlic for 1 minute over medium heat, adding more fat if necessary. Cover the skillet, lower the heat, and simmer for 5 minutes, shaking the pan now and then. Transfer the mushrooms to the ovenproof dish with the onions and carrots.

Brown the sausages in the same skillet over high heat for 1 minute or so and add them to the mushrooms, onions, and carrots.

On a plate, season the flour with a large pinch of salt and freshly ground pepper. Dip the kidney in flour and brown for 2–3 minutes, adding more fat if necessary. Transfer the kidney to the dish with the sausages, mushrooms, carrots, and onions.

In the same skillet, bring the cream to a boil, stirring all the while to incorporate the drippings at the bottom of the pan. Transfer to a small mixing bowl with the tarragon. Cover and reserve for the end.

Add the hard-boiled eggs, the olives, and the chicken pieces, skin side up, along with their juices from the plate, to the dish with the kidney, sausages, mushrooms, onions, and carrots.

Season with salt and freshly ground pepper and add thyme. Set aside.

Roll out the pastry to a circle about 1 inch wider than the top of the dish. Refrigerate on a cookie sheet for 15 minutes or until the pastry is firm but not stiff.

Brush the rim and the outside of the dish with the egg yolk glaze.

Cover the pot with the pastry and seal it, pushing the dough around the outside of the rim. Preheat the oven to 400 degrees.

Lightly brush egg glaze on top of the pastry and bake in the middle of the oven for 45 minutes.

Just before serving, bring the reserved cream with tarragon to a boil. Discard the tarragon.

To serve: Cut the dough into 6 wedges; the pastry is very brittle, so do the best you can to place a wedge on each plate. Then pour the boiling cream over the chicken and serve the chicken and other filling spooned over the pie shell. Remove and discard the carcass pieces before serving, or take them as the cook's reward.

The pie can be prepared in advance and refrigerated overnight, unglazed. Refrigerate and reserve the remaining egg glaze. Remove the chicken pie from the refrigerator about 30 minutes before baking. Brush with the egg glaze and bake as above.

note

chicken marengo

To celebrate Napoleon's victory at Marengo, in Italy, his chef created a dish à l'italienne.

SERVES 4

One 3-pound chicken
3 tablespoons flour
Salt
Freshly ground black pepper
2 tablespoons olive oil
1 cup thinly sliced onion
1 tablespoon minced garlic
1/2 pound white mushrooms
1 tablespoon butter
1 cup Tomato Sauce (page 6)
1/3 cup white wine, preferably chardonnay
10 unpitted niçoise olives

Ask the butcher to cut the chicken into drumsticks, thighs, breast, and wings, and the carcass into several pieces. Trim and discard the fat around the chicken pieces.

On a plate, season the flour with a large pinch of salt and freshly ground pepper.

Heat the oil in a 5 1/2-quart Dutch oven over moderate heat. Dip the chicken, including the carcass pieces, in flour, a few pieces at a time, and brown all over, skin side down first. Transfer the chicken to a plate; season with salt and freshly ground pepper. Set aside.

Reserve 2 tablespoons fat in the pot (or add more oil, if necessary). Add the onion, garlic, and 2 tablespoons water. Cover and simmer for 5 minutes over low heat. Reserve.

Cut off the stems of the mushrooms and chop them. In a small pan, combine the stems with 1 cup water, 1 tablespoon butter, and a large pinch of salt. Bring to a boil and reduce by half. Strain and reserve the mushroom broth, discarding the solids.

Add the tomato sauce, wine, and mushroom broth to the onions. Bring to a boil and boil for 1 minute, stirring with a wooden spoon.Cut the mushroom caps into small wedges.

Turn down the heat and add the chicken pieces skin side up along with their juices gathered in the plate, the mushrooms, and the olives.

Cover the Dutch oven and simmer gently for 45 minutes. Now and then, uncover and let the water condensation fall back into the pot.

Transfer the chicken to a heated platter and discard the carcass pieces. Cover with foil and reserve. Degrease the pan juices, following the instructions on page xiv, if necessary. Serve the juices separately in a sauceboat.

variation:
veal marengo

Substitute 2 pounds boned veal shoulder, cut into 2-inch pieces. Braise for 1 hour or until tender.

chicken à l'étouffée

À l'étouffée means "smothered." The chicken is nested in the vegetables and cooked with a very small amount of liquid. The chicken stays moist and browns lightly. With this type of braising, I seal the pot, following the directions on page xv.

SERVES 4

One 3-pound chicken
3 parsley sprigs
Salt
Freshly ground black pepper
2 tablespoons olive oil
1 large Yukon Gold potato, peeled and cut into 2-inch cubes
4 medium carrots, peeled, cut into 1-inch slices
2 cups onions, peeled and each cut into eighths
4 garlic cloves, coarsely chopped
1 teaspoon dried thyme or oregano
1 large fresh bay leaf

Remove the cluster of fat found in the cavity of the chicken. Stuff the parsley inside the bird and sprinkle with salt and freshly ground pepper. Chop the fat and reserve 2 tablespoons or, if there is none, use an additional 2 tablespoons olive oil. Discard the remaining fat.

Drizzle 1 tablespoon olive oil in a 5 1/2-quart Dutch oven; add the vegetables, garlic, and chicken fat; sprinkle with salt, freshly ground pepper, and thyme. Mix well. Pour 1/2 cup water over the vegetables.

Nest the chicken in the vegetables. Drizzle 1 more tablespoon of oil over the chicken. The dish can be prepared 2 or 3 hours ahead of time up to this step.

Preheat the oven to 350 degrees.

Place the bay leaf on top of the chicken, cover tightly, and seal the pot, following the directions on page xv, or add 1/4 cup water now and then while cooking.

Bake in the middle of the oven for 2 hours.

Break the seal (if you used one) in the kitchen. Transfer the chicken to a large heated platter and garnish with the vegetables. Carve at the table.

braised quail with apricots

The sauce makes this dish. The quail are first slowly roasted, then braised with apricots and seasoned with curry and nutmeg. Choose California dried apricots—not the Turkish variety, which are too sweet and without flavor.

SERVES 4

8 dried California apricots
1/2 cup port
8 whole quail
Salt
Freshly ground black pepper
2 lemons
4 tablespoons olive oil
1 cup sliced onions
1 medium carrot, cut into 1/4-inch-thick slices
1/8 teaspoon grated nutmeg
1 teaspoon mild or hot curry
1 fresh sprig rosemary
1 bay leaf
1/2 cup homemade or commercial chicken stock
8 small leeks, white part only

Soak the apricots in the port in a small bowl while preparing the quail.

Pat the quail dry with paper towels. Sprinkle with salt and pepper inside and out.

With a vegetable peeler, slice off the peel of the 2 lemons. Chop the peel and add half to the cavities. Set aside the remaining peel for later. Tie the quail with string, tying the wings and breast together and tying the legs with the bottom of the carcass.

In a 5 1/2-quart Dutch oven, heat the oil over medium-low heat. Brown the quail evenly, turning them over once in a while during the browning process, adjusting the heat if necessary. The browning will take about 20 minutes.

Transfer the quail to a plate. Add the onions, the remaining lemon peel, and the carrots to the hot fat and stir with a wooden spoon for 5 minutes until lightly browned.

Replace the quail in the pot, breast side up, and place one apricot on each quail. Season with salt, freshly ground black pepper, nutmeg, and curry. Add the rosemary, bay leaf, port from the apricots, and chicken stock. Cover the pot.

Simmer the quail over moderate heat for 40 minutes. Now and then, uncover the pot, let the water condensation on the underside of lid fall back in the pot, and baste the top of the quail with a spoon.

In a small saucepan, cover the leeks with salted water and bring to a slow boil. Boil 5 minutes or until the leeks are just tender (use the point of a knife blade to judge their doneness). Strain the leeks gently, trying not to break them up too much, and transfer them to a heated platter. Cover with foil and reserve in a warm place.

Transfer the quail to the platter, re-cover with foil, and reserve. Degrease the cooking juices if necessary. Serve the quail with the leeks on the side, and pass the cooking juices in a sauceboat.

on rabbits

I ask the butcher to cut a rabbit in several pieces: the saddle cut crosswise into 3 pieces and the hind legs cut into 2 pieces each. Those are the pieces I cook when I have guests. I freeze the front legs and rib cage, which are very bony but delicious—I keep them for a family dinner.

rabbit alibaba

When I have unexpected guests for dinner, I often cook this rabbit dish or Braise of Pork Roast with Onions (page 67). It's easy to prepare, involves no fuss, and is always a hit. The rabbit pieces are coated in olive oil in a Dutch oven with onions and garlic, braised in a cup of white wine, and seasoned with rosemary and sage.

One 3-pound rabbit, cut into several pieces (see above)
$^1/_4$ cup olive oil
$^1/_2$ cup chopped onion
2 garlic cloves, peeled and chopped fine
$1^1/_2$ tablespoons tomato paste
1 cup white wine, preferably Chardonnay
Salt
$^1/_4$ teaspoon hot red pepper flakes
1 sprig fresh rosemary
4 fresh sage leaves or a small cluster

SERVES 4 TO 6

Coat the rabbit pieces with the oil in a $5^1/_2$-quart Dutch oven.

Scatter the onion and garlic over the rabbit.

Combine the tomato paste and wine together; pour over the rabbit.

Season the rabbit with salt and hot pepper flakes; add the herbs. Cover tightly and cook over moderate heat for 1 hour, turning the rabbit pieces over once.

Uncover, raise the heat, and boil down until the juices become slightly syrupy, turning the rabbit pieces over in the syrupy sauce.

rabbit with prunes soaked in port

This dish is very popular in the Flemish part of Belgium and is one of my favorite ways to cook rabbit. I always have prunes marinating in port; it's one of my staples. I serve mashed potatoes, a perfect accompaniment, with this dish.

SERVES 4

$^1\!/_2$ cup Prunes Marinated in Port with Orange Zest (page 12) with $^1\!/_3$ cup port syrup, or $^1\!/_2$ cup prunes soaked in 1 cup port overnight
3 tablespoons flour
Salt
Freshly ground pepper
3 tablespoons vegetable oil
One 3-pound rabbit, cut into several pieces (page 103)
$^1\!/_2$ cup coarsely chopped shallots
1 cup red wine, Côtes-du-Rhône or Zinfandel

Soak prunes in port overnight if you do not have prunes already marinated in port.

Season the flour with a large pinch of salt and freshly ground pepper. Heat the oil in a $5^1\!/_2$-quart Dutch oven over medium-high heat. Dip the rabbit pieces in the flour and brown evenly.

Scatter the shallots around the rabbit. Season with salt and freshly ground pepper.

Add the wine, the prunes, and the port syrup from the prunes. Cover tightly and simmer over medium-low heat. Now and then, let the water condensation on the underside of the lid fall back into the pot, and turn over the rabbit pieces with tongs.

Transfer the rabbit and prunes to a heated platter and reserve in a warm place. Boil down the juices just enough to be sure they are slightly syrupy. Serve in a sauceboat.

squab en cocotte

This dish is a classic in France, squab roasted and braised in a cocotte (a Dutch oven) with fresh peas.

SERVES 4

2 tablespoons butter
1 tablespoon olive oil
6 ounces slab bacon or pancetta, cut into $1/4$-inch-thick slices, then crosswise into $1/2$-inch strips
4 boneless squabs, about 10 ounces each
2 pounds fresh peas in their pods, shelled (about 2 cups)
Salt
Freshly ground black pepper
2 sprigs fresh thyme

In a $5^1/2$-quart Dutch oven, melt the butter with the oil over moderate heat. Add the bacon or pancetta and cook, stirring with a wooden spoon now and then, until very lightly brown. Transfer the pancetta to a plate and reserve.

Gently brown the squabs evenly on all sides, breast side down first, over moderate heat. It will take about 20 minutes to brown the birds. Remember that the fat at the bottom of the pan must not burn. Transfer the birds to the plate with the pancetta.

Pour the fat into a small bowl and cool for 1 minute or so. Spoon out the clear fat and put back into the pot. Discard the brown residue at the bottom of the bowl.

Heat the fat over medium heat and transfer the squabs back into the Dutch oven, breast side up. Scatter the pancetta and the peas around the birds. Season with salt and freshly ground pepper and add the thyme. Cover tightly and braise the birds for 35 minutes over gentle heat. Now and then, uncover the pot, and let the water condensation on the underside of the lid fall back in the pot.

Carve the birds into 4 pieces each, transfer them with the bacon or pancetta to a heated platter, and decorate with the peas. Ladle the pan juices and fat over the birds.

pheasant on a bed of braised cabbage

Braising cabbage and bacon with any sort of meat, poultry, or game is perfect for a winter-night dinner. Pheasant are not very fatty—that is why I use so much fat. If chicken or guinea hens are braised in the same manner, cut down on the fat.

SERVES 4

6 ounces slab bacon
2 tablespoons butter
1 tablespoon olive oil
Salt
Freshly ground black pepper
One 3-pound pheasant (Ask the butcher to cut the pheasant into several pieces: thighs, legs, the breast cut into 2 pieces, and the carcass chopped into several pieces.)
2 cups thinly sliced onions
One 2-pound white cabbage
1½ pounds small Yukon Gold potatoes, peeled
2 tablespoons minced fresh parsley

Discard the rind of the bacon and trim the fat. Cut the bacon into ¼-inch-thick slices, then crosswise into ½-inch pieces, called "lardons."

Melt the butter and oil in a 5½-quart Dutch oven over moderate heat and brown the bacon until light golden; transfer to a plate and reserve.

Pour the fat into a small bowl; cool and spoon out the clear fat into the Dutch oven, discarding the brown residue at the bottom of the bowl.

Heat the clear fat over moderate heat and brown the pheasant pieces, turning over occasionally. Transfer the pheasant to a plate.

Add the onions to the fat and add ¼ cup water. Cover tightly and cook for 10 minutes.

Put the bacon and the pheasant pieces back into the Dutch oven on top of the onions. Sprinkle with salt and freshly ground pepper.

Cover tightly and simmer over moderate heat for 45 minutes. Now and then, uncover and let the water condensation on the underside of the lid fall back into the pot.

Meanwhile, discard the tough dark green outer leaves of the cabbage. Quarter the cabbage and cut out the center core. Slice the cabbage into ½-inch strips (it makes about 10 cups).

Bring 5 quarts of salted water to a boil in a stockpot; add the cabbage and cover the pot. Bring back to a boil for 5 minutes.

Drain the cabbage in a colander set in the kitchen sink. Cool.

Season the cabbage with salt and pepper and add it to the pheasant for the last 20 minutes of cooking.

In a seperate saucepan, cover the potatoes with cold salted water and cook for 20 minutes or until tender. Drain. Serve the potatoes with the pheasant and cabbage.

variation:
duck confit with braised cabbage

Duck Confit (page 108)
One 2-pound white cabbage
1½ pounds small Yukon Gold potatoes, peeled

Preheat the oven to 200 degrees.

Place the crock with the confit in the middle of the oven to melt the fat slowly. With tongs, lift out the duck pieces from the fat. The fat can be reused for another confit.

Heat a large skillet over medium heat and sear the duck until golden brown.

Reserve 2 tablespoons fat in the skillet, add the reserved parboiled cabbage (see main recipe opposite), place the duck on top, cover, and braise for 20 minutes.

Serve with potatoes (see main recipe).

duck confit

In the fall, there is feverish activity in the farms of southwest France, making foie gras and confit for the long winter months ahead. Confit is duck or goose legs and necks cooked and preserved in their own fat. On the farms, there is no need for refrigeration; the confit is kept in cool cellars in small glazed crocks.

Goose fat is easily found in upscale gourmet shops or catalogs, or you can render your own.

FOR 4 LEGS AND 4 THIGHS (ASK THE BUTCHER TO SEPARATE THE LEGS FROM THE THIGHS)

2 tablespoons coarse sea salt
4 garlic cloves, minced
$^1/_2$ tablespoon fresh thyme leaves
2 pounds goose fat

Combine the salt, garlic, and thyme and rub the duck pieces with the mixture. Place in a large container and cover. Refrigerate for 3–4 days.

With a towel, rub the salt off the duck pieces.

Preheat the oven to 220 degrees.

In a 4-quart Dutch oven or a pot just large enough to hold the duck, melt the fat over low heat. Bury the duck pieces in the melted fat. They should be covered with the fat. Bake in the oven for 2 hours or until very tender. Test with the blade of a knife, which should pierce the duck easily.

Let cool for several hours. With tongs, remove the duck pieces and stack them in a large crock. Pour the fat carefully over the duck pieces, covering them totally with fat. Store in the refrigerator.

To use the confit for cassoulet or for brasing cabbage with confit:

Preheat the oven to 150 degrees.

Place the crock with the confit in the middle of the oven to melt the fat slowly; this will take several hours. With tongs, lift out the duck pieces from the fat and drain on a baking rack fitted over a large plate. The fat can be reused for another confit.

spicy ducks à la créole

In Madagascar, the French island off South Africa, spices are used abundantly in most dishes, which is practically unheard of in France. Asian, French, and Indian influences are present in the cooking there. Rice is the accompaniment to all dishes from the island.

SERVES 6

Two 4-pound ducks (Ask the butcher to cut the ducks into several pieces: legs, thighs, wings, the breast cut into 2 pieces, and the carcass chopped into several pieces.)
1 tablespoon olive oil
Salt
1/2 cup minced onions
1 tablespoon minced garlic
5 peppercorns
4 whole cloves
1 teaspoon turmeric
1/8 teaspoon ground nutmeg
1/8 teaspoon ground cinnamon
1 tablespoon minced fresh ginger
1 tablespoon flour
One 14-ounce can Italian plum tomatoes, chopped
1/4 cup red wine, Zinfandel or Côtes-du-Rhône

Trim off the fat from each piece of duck, even scraping off the fat between the skin and the meat wherever possible. Prick the skin of the duck all over with a skewer or the point of a knife.

In a large skillet, heat the olive oil over medium heat. Brown the duck pieces evenly, a few pieces at a time, turning occasionally. Brown the carcass to add flavor to the cooking juices; it will be discarded before serving. Transfer the duck to a 5 1/2-quart Dutch oven and sprinkle with salt.

Reserve 2 tablespoons fat in the skillet. Add the onions, garlic, 2 tablespoons water, and all the spices and stir. Lower the heat, cover, and cook over moderate heat for 10 minutes.

Uncover, sprinkle with the flour, and stir for a few seconds. Add the tomatoes and their juice to the mixture, cover, and simmer for 15 minutes, again over moderate heat.

Uncover, raise the heat, add the wine, and bring to a boil. Pour the mixture over the duck and cover.

Simmer the duck over moderate heat for 2 hours or until tender. Now and then, uncover the pot and let the water condensation on the underside of the lid fall back into the pot.

Transfer the duck to a heated platter and cover with foil. Reserve in a warm place. Discard the carcass pieces or keep them to nibble on.

To degrease the sauce, follow the directions on page xiv. Ladle some of the sauce over the duck and serve with the remaining sauce on the side. Serve rice as an accompaniment.

venison stew

Choose either the shank or shoulder of venison for this stew, and reserve the leg for a roast. The meat should marinate for at least two days to intermingle the flavors of meat and marinade. If you don't have that much time, then skip the first step. When I make this stew, I bake a corn pudding; stew and pudding are made for each other.

SERVES 6

4 pounds boneless venison shank or shoulder, cut into 2-inch cubes
1 large carrot, cut into 1/2-inch slices
1 small onion, quartered
Salt
Freshly ground black pepper
2 sprigs fresh thyme
2 sprigs fresh rosemary
1 bottle (750 ml) red wine, Zinfandel or Côtes-du-Rhône
1 tablespoon red wine vinegar
4 tablespoons flour
4 tablespoons olive oil or more

For the corn pudding:
3/4 cup stone-ground yellow cornmeal
1 1/2 cups milk
4 tablespoons butter
4 eggs
One 16-ounce can cream-style corn

In a large mixing bowl, toss together the meat, carrots, and onions. Season with salt and freshly ground pepper; add thyme, rosemary, wine, and vinegar. Cover the bowl and refrigerate for 2 days, turning the meat over 2 or 3 times during that period.

Drain the meat, vegetables, and herbs in a large sieve over a bowl; sort out the vegetables and herbs and set them aside for later in a small mixing bowl. Reserve the liquid.

In a bowl, season 2 tablespoons of flour with salt and freshly ground pepper. Pat the meat dry with paper towels.

In a large skillet, heat 2 tablespoons oil over medium-high heat. Dip the meat in the flour a few pieces at a time and brown evenly, turning the meat over to brown on all sides. Add more oil if necessary. Transfer the meat to a 5 1/2-quart Dutch oven; sprinkle with salt and freshly ground pepper.

Sauté the reserved vegetables in the same skillet, adding more fat if necessary. Add to the meat.

In the same skillet, heat 2 tablespoons olive oil (if there is no oil left over), and whisk in 2 tablespoons flour over moderate heat; switch to a wooden spoon and stir constantly until the mixture is hazelnut-colored.

Over high heat, whisk in the reserved wine marinade and bring to a light boil. Strain the boiling liquid over the meat, and place the reserved herbs on top.

Place a piece of parchment paper directly over the meat and cover tightly with the lid. Bring to a boil then reduce the heat to a gentle simmer and cook for 3 hours. Now and then, peek under the parchment paper and stir the meat in the sauce.

For the pudding:

Preheat the oven to 350 degrees.

Season the cornmeal with salt in a medium mixing bowl.

Bring the milk and butter to a boil.

Whisk the milk into the cornmeal and add the corn. Set aside.

Beat the eggs in a heavy-duty mixer until they are thick and pale yellow.

Whisk the beaten eggs into the cornmeal mixture. Sprinkle with freshly ground pepper; taste and add more salt if necessary.

Pour the mixture into a buttered 2-quart oval or rectangular ovenproof baking dish. Cover with a buttered piece of parchment paper. The pudding can be prepared ahead of time and refrigerated; see note.

Bake the corn pudding 30 minutes before the venison stew is ready.

Remove the meat and vegetables and transfer to a heated serving dish; cover with foil and keep warm.

To degrease and finish the sauce, follow the directions on page xiv. Ladle some of the sauce over the venison and pass the remaining sauce separately. Serve the corn pudding on the side.

note

The stew can be prepared 2 to 3 days ahead. Refrigerate the meat and sauce in separate containers. Bring to room temperature and reheat while baking the corn pudding.

braised ducks with young turnips

When turnips are young and firm in the early spring and early fall, try this classic dish.

Two 4-pound ducks (Ask the butcher to cut the duck into several pieces: legs, thighs, wings, the breast cut into 2 pieces, and the carcass in several pieces.)
1 tablespoon olive oil
Salt
Freshly ground black pepper
2 tablespoons flour
2 cups homemade or commercial chicken stock
1 large sprig fresh thyme and 3 sprigs of parsley tied together
2 tablespoons butter
1 pound young white baby turnips, peeled
1 teaspoon sugar

Trim off the fat from each piece of duck, even scraping off the fat between the skin and the meat wherever possible. Prick the skin of the duck all over with a skewer or the point of a knife.

Heat 1 tablespoon oil in a large skillet over medium heat. Brown the duck evenly, a few pieces at a time. Brown the carcass to add flavor to the cooking juices. Transfer the duck to a 5^1/$_2$-quart Dutch oven and season with salt and freshly ground pepper.

Reserve 3 tablespoons of the fat in the skillet and reheat over moderate heat. Whisk the fat with the flour until the mixture is smooth. Switch to a wooden spoon and stir the mixture constantly until it turns the color of hazelnut, adjusting the heat if necessary (this will take about 5 minutes).

Pour the chicken stock into the skillet and bring to a boil, whisking constantly, for 1 minute; then add to the duck. Place the bouquet of thyme and parsley on top; cover with greased parchment paper and the lid. Simmer over moderate heat for 2 hours or until tender. Now and then, peek under the paper and let the water condensed on the underside of the lid fall back in the pot.

Meanwhile, melt the butter in a nonstick skillet and add the baby turnips; sprinkle with sugar, salt, and freshly ground pepper. Sauté for 5 minutes over medium heat, shaking the pan once in a while.

Add the turnips to the duck for the last 20 minutes of cooking. Transfer the duck and turnips to a heated platter, discard the carcass pieces, and cover the platter with foil. Set aside in a warm place.

Degrease the sauce, following the directions on page xiv. Ladle some of the sauce over the ducks and serve the rest in a sauceboat.

fish

Unlike meat, seafood doesn't gain flavor from long slow cooking. When fish is overcooked, it becomes flavorless and uninteresting. That's why the fish and shellfish preparations in this chapter require a short baking or braising time. Still, some preparation can be done ahead, so that when it is time to cook for dinner, many of the more time-consuming steps are already out of the way.

The addition of wine, cream, olive oil, or butter enhances the natural flavor of the fish. Cream marries well with any fish, but these days, most of us who are health-conscious tend to shun it. If that applies to you, you might try Oyster Chowder (page 131), whose shellfish liquor is enough to provide plenty of flavor; or Cioppino (page 135), the California dish that gets its flavor from a spicy tomato stew.

I've put Paella in this chapter even though besides prawns, shrimp, cockles (or clams), and mussels, it includes pork and chicken cooked with the rice. When most of us think of paella we do visualize a beautiful array of shellfish—which is, in fact, the most prominent feature of the dish.

Rice and pasta are my favorite accompaniments for all these dishes.

daube of tuna

A daube is a meat or fish stew from southeastern France. To keep braised tuna moist is a feat. Richard Olney, in the Time-Life cookbooks, had a technique: he larded tuna with anchovies; layered it between tomatoes, onions, sorrel, and salad leaves; and braised it in a medium-hot oven. All the work is done ahead of time; at dinnertime, it is just a matter of baking the tuna in the oven. This is my favorite fish casserole for summer and autumn. If you have a garden, plant sorrel among the herbs; it has a lemony tartness that marries well with fish and veal. After each clipping, it grows back fast and needs no attending to. You can use arugula instead, but it's a poor substitute.

SERVES 4

12 anchovy fillets in salt brine or oil
One 2½-pound tuna steak (8 inches in diameter and 2 inches thick)
Butter to grease the pan
Several leaves of Boston lettuce, washed and dried
4 ounces sorrel (sour grass) leaves, washed, stems discarded, and cut into julienne strips
2 medium onions, peeled and sliced into ⅛-inch-thick rings
4 juicy medium tomatoes (not plum tomatoes) peeled and sliced thin
Salt
Freshly ground black pepper
¼ cup white wine, preferably Chardonnay

For saffron rice:
1 cup homemade or commercial chicken stock, or water
2 tablespoons butter plus butter for the baking dish
Large pinch of saffron strands
Salt
Freshly ground black pepper
1 cup long-grain rice

Wash the anchovy fillets under cold running water. Pat dry with paper towels.

Make 12 incisions in the tuna with a small, sharp knife; insert a fillet of anchovy in each incision. Preheat the oven to 325 degrees.

Butter a deep 3-quart ovenproof dish. Line the bottom and sides of the pan with lettuce leaves. Layer half the sorrel, onion rings, and tomato slices on top of the lettuce. Lightly season with salt and pepper (remember that the anchovies are salty).

Place the tuna on top of the vegetables and cover it with the remaining tomatoes, onion, and sorrel. Finally, top with more lettuce leaves and pour the wine over the dish.

Cover (the dish can be prepared ahead of time to this step).

Bake the tuna for 1 hour in the middle of the oven.

Meanwhile, prepare the rice. In a 2-quart saucepan, heat the stock or water with the butter and saffron.

Put the rice in a small buttered ovenproof baking dish and pour the liquid over it; sprinkle with salt and freshly ground pepper. Cover and bake with the fish for the last 30 minutes. Fluff the rice with a fork and serve.

monkfish with tagliatelle

Monkfish is a perfect fish to braise, as its flesh does not become mushy from long cooking. I make this dish only in the summer, when fresh tomatoes are in season. I serve the monkfish on a bed of lemony tagliatelle. It's a grand dish. Some of the work can be done 1 hour before finishing the dish for dinner.

SERVES 4

2 pounds monkfish, in one large fillet, preferably a center piece
2 garlic cloves, peeled and cut into 10 slivers
1 pound fresh tomatoes
2 tablespoons butter
1 large carrot, peeled, quartered, and cut into 2-inch-long sticks
2 large shallots, peeled and halved
Salt
Freshly ground black pepper
2 sprigs fresh thyme, one 10-inch-long celery stalk, and 1 bay leaf, all tied together
1/3 cup white wine, preferably Chardonnay
6 ounces dried tagliatelle
1/3 cup heavy cream
1/8 teaspoon saffron threads
1 tablespoon olive oil
2 tablespoons freshly squeezed lemon juice
1 tablespoon grated lemon peel

With the point of a sharp knife, make incisions in the monkfish and bury the slivers of garlic.

Meanwhile, bring 2 quarts of water to a boil. Pour it over the tomatoes and wait 15 seconds before peeling them. Slice the tomatoes in half horizontally, and with your thumb discard the seeds. Chop the tomatoes—you should have about 1 1/3 cups. Reserve. These steps can be done the morning of the day you plan on serving.

In a 4-quart Dutch oven, melt the butter over medium heat. Add the monkfish and cook for 5 minutes, turning the fish over several times and adjusting the heat to avoid burning the butter.

Scatter the carrots and shallots around the fish. Season with salt and freshly ground pepper. Place the tied herbs on top of the fish. Cover tightly and simmer gently for 10 minutes.

Add the wine and continue braising for another 15 minutes, turning the fish over once or twice and basting it at the same time.

Meanwhile, bring 5 quarts of salted water to a boil in a large pot. Drop the pasta into the boiling water and cook until just under al dente (about 8 minutes)

While the pasta is cooking, transfer the fish with the carrots and shallots to a heated platter, cover with foil, and reserve in a warm oven. Discard the thyme, celery, and bay leaf. Add the cream, saffron, and chopped tomatoes to the braising liquid in the pot and bring to a boil over very high heat. Boil the sauce down until it starts to thicken just slightly.

Drain the pasta and toss it in a heated bowl with the oil, lemon juice, and rind. Season with salt and pepper to taste.

To serve: Bone the fish, cutting alongside the central bone, and cut it into 4 pieces.

Divide the pasta among 4 plates, and place a piece of monkfish on top with several carrot sticks and shallots. Ladle the sauce over the fish and serve immediately.

choucroute with seafood

Traditionally, cabbage is shredded and put in brine toward the end of summer; as the months go by, the sauerkraut gets more acidic. Young sauerkraut, however, is sweet, light, and easy to digest—a perfect accompaniment to this seafood dish, which is considerably lighter than the meat version, Choucroute Garnie (page 80).

FOR 6

2 pounds sauerkraut
3 tablespoons olive oil
1 cup finely chopped onions
1 tablespoon juniper berries
1 tablespoon sugar
Salt
Freshly ground black pepper
1 bottle (750 ml) white wine, preferably Chardonnay
12 small potatoes, peeled
2 teaspoons mild curry
1½ pounds halibut steak or any similar white fish
18 large sea scallops (with the coral if possible)

For the sauce:
¼ cup minced shallots
1 tablespoon white vinegar
1 teaspoon mustard
1 teaspoon horseradish
1 cup heavy cream

Wash the sauerkraut several times in cold water. Turn it into a 7¼-quart Dutch oven and cover with cold water. Bring to a rolling boil; turn off the heat, drain in a colander set in the kitchen sink, and reserve.

In the same pot, heat the oil over medium-low heat and add the onions and ¼ cup water; cook, stirring, for 5 minutes, wilting the onions.

Add the drained sauerkraut and stir in the juniper berries; sprinkle with sugar, salt, and freshly ground pepper and stir once more. Pour in 2½ cups of the wine, reserving the remaining ½ cup for the sauce. Cover tightly and simmer gently for 45 minutes.

Peel the potatoes and reserve in water. After 45 minutes, add the potatoes to the sauerkraut and simmer for another 15 minutes.

Sprinkle curry and salt over the seafood, cover, and reserve until serving. The dish can be prepared ahead of time through this step.

Reheat the sauerkraut with the potatoes at a low simmer for at least 20 minutes.

Place the seafood on top of the sauerkraut. Cover and poach over gentle heat for about 10–15 minutes, turning once during the cooking.

Meanwhile, prepare the sauce: Combine the shallots, vinegar, and reserved wine in a heavy-bottomed saucepan. Bring the mixture to a boil and stir until the wine and vinegar have evaporated. Add the mustard, horseradish, and cream; bring back to a gentle boil until the sauce thickens (about 5 minutes); taste, and adjust seasoning with salt and pepper. Serve it in a sauceboat with the sauerkraut, fish, and potatoes.

salmon papillotes

Cooking fish in papillote, or paper, is another form of braising. The salmon fillets and tomato slices are wrapped in parchment paper or aluminum foil; they can be prepared several hours ahead before being baked in a hot oven for 15 minutes. Serve the papillotes as is, in their paper shell. Or, for a more elegant presentation during the late spring and summer when sorrel is available, transfer them to a platter and serve a sorrel sauce on the side. Sorrel sauce with salmon was made famous 40 years ago by the Troisgros brothers, who have an exquisite restaurant in Roanne, in the middle of nowhere in France. If you cannot find sorrel, just skip the sauce; it is interesting only with sorrel, which has a very sharp lemony flavor.

SERVES 4

Four 6-ounce salmon fillets
2 medium tomatoes cut into $1/4$-inch slices
4 tablespoons olive oil
$1/2$ cup white vermouth
Salt
Freshly ground black pepper

Optional:
$1/2$ cup shredded sorrel (sour grass)
$1/2$ cup heavy cream

Cut 4 pieces of parchment paper or aluminum foil large enough to wrap each salmon fillet (about 15 by 11 inches). Drizzle $1/2$ tablespoon oil over the bottom of each piece of paper and place a salmon fillet, skin side down, on each. Cover the fillets with tomato slices; dribble $1/2$ tablespoon oil and 2 tablespoons dry vermouth on top of the tomato slices. Sprinkle with salt and freshly ground pepper.

Wrap the fillets in the paper, folding the top and sides of the parchment to prevent any liquid from escaping.

Place the papillotes on a broiler pan. You can prepare the papillotes through this step in advance and refrigerate them for up to several hours, but bring them back to room temperature before baking.

Preheat the oven to 450 degrees.

Bake in the middle of the oven for 15 minutes.

Open the papillotes and test to see if the salmon is cooked through by poking a matchstick through the fish. There should be no resistance. Remember: If you put more than 4 papillotes in the oven, they will take a bit longer to cook.

Serve each papillote on a heated plate.

For a more elegant presentation: Wash the sorrel and fold each leaf in half with one hand. With the other hand, tear out the stems and the center vein of the leaves. Wash and dry. Stack the leaves and cut them in $1/8$-inch strips (julienne). This can be done after the papillotes are prepared for baking.

Bake the papillotes as directed above. Make a hole in each papillote and drain the cooking juices into a skillet. Open up 1 papillote at a time and gently transfer it with 2 flat steel spatulas to a heated platter. Reserve in a warm oven.

Add the cream to the cooking juices and bring to a boil. Add the sorrel and stir with a wooden spatula until the sorrel melts (about 1 to 2 minutes). Taste the sauce, adjust the seasoning, ladle it over the fish, and serve right away.

kedgeree

Sometimes called khicharhi, this dish originated in India and was brought to England by the British colonials, who served it for breakfast. It is a casserole of cooked salmon and rice, seasoned with curry and nutmeg and baked in either a white sauce or cream. You can prepare it on Saturday and bake it for Sunday brunch. For a complete meal, add cooked vegetables such as peas, broccoli, or zucchini to the casserole.

SERVES 6

1½ pounds fresh salmon fillet
½ cup white wine, preferably Chardonnay
1½ cups coarsely chopped onions
5 sprigs parsley
Salt
5 peppercorns
3 tablespoons unsalted butter
¾ cup short-grain rice
2 eggs
2 tablespoons freshly squeezed lemon or lime juice
2 teaspoons mild or hot curry
¼ teaspoon grated nutmeg
1 cup heavy cream

Cover the fish with the wine and 3 cups water in a 4-quart pan. Add ½ cup of the chopped onions and the parsley stems. Chop the parsley leaves and reserve for later. Sprinkle the fish with salt and add the peppercorns. Cover and bring the fish to a slow boil. Lower the heat and simmer for 20 minutes or until the fish is totally cooked. You can tell by plunging a wooden matchstick into the center of the fillet. There should be no resistance. Cool the fish in the liquid.

Transfer the fish to a plate. Strain the poaching liquid, about 2 cups, and reserve it for later. Discard the skin and small bones and flake the salmon with two forks. It makes about 2 cups. Reserve.

In a 3-quart pan, melt 3 tablespoons butter and stir in the remaining cup of chopped onions. Cook until honey-colored, stirring once in a while and adding 2–3 tablespoons water if the onions start coloring too fast.

Wash the rice under cold running water. Drain thoroughly and add to the onions. Stir for a minute or so; sprinkle with salt and pour in the reserved salmon poaching liquid. Bring to a boil, adjust the heat to a low simmer, cover the pot tightly, and cook for 20 minutes or until the rice is cooked.

Meanwhile, bring 2 quarts of water to a boil; gently lower 2 eggs into the water and boil slowly for 10 minutes. Drain off the water and run cold water over the eggs. Peel and chop the eggs. Reserve.

In a large mixing bowl, combine the salmon, rice, eggs, and reserved chopped parsley; sprinkle with lemon or lime juice, curry, and nutmeg. Taste and adjust the amount of spices to your liking.

Add the cream to the salmon and rice and mix. Taste and adjust seasoning if necessary.

Transfer the kedgeree into a buttered deep 3-quart ovenproof dish and cover with buttered parchment paper. The kedgeree can be prepared ahead of time through this step, but bring it back to room temperature before baking.

Preheat the oven to 325 degrees.

Bake in the middle of the oven for 20 minutes.

Serve immediately.

salt cod à la florentine

I love salt cod, and I was enchanted by a casserole of creamy salt cod baked on top a layer of spinach that I had with friends at a restaurant in Provence. *À la Florentine* is a term used for a dish made with spinach. Remember that salt cod must be soaked in fresh water before cooking; the amount of time depends on how it was cured. To be safe, I soak it for 36 hours.

SERVES 4 FOR A MAIN COURSE, 6 FOR A FIRST COURSE

1 pound salt cod
2 cups milk
2 tablespoons olive oil
1/2 cup minced shallots or onions
1 teaspoon minced garlic
Freshly ground black pepper
2 pounds loose spinach (not baby spinach), or 3 10-ounce bags fresh spinach
Salt
2 cups White Sauce (page 5)
1/2 cup grated Gruyère cheese

Under cold running water, wash the salt off the surface of the cod. Put the cod in a large mixing bowl of cold water in the sink under trickling running water for 1 hour. Refrigerate in the bowl, covered with cold water, for 36 hours, changing the water every so often, about 4 times.

Drain the cod and wash once more under cold running water. Put it in a 3-quart pot and cover with milk. Cover the pot and bring the milk to a near-boil; lower the heat and poach for 15 minutes. Drain the cod and discard the milk. Remove and discard the cod's skin and bones. Flake the flesh with the tines of a fork and reserve.

In a 4-quart Dutch oven, heat the oil over medium heat and stir in the minced shallots or onions and garlic with 1/4 cup water. Cover and simmer for 5 minutes. Add the cod; sprinkle with freshly ground pepper; cover and braise over a low simmer for 5 minutes. Turn off the heat and reserve.

To clean the spinach: Fill the sink with warm water and plunge the spinach into the water. Swish the spinach in the water to loosen the grit. Remove the stems by folding each spinach leaf vertically in one hand and tearing off the stem with the other hand. Discard the stems. Transfer the spinach to a large bowl. Do not dry the spinach—the water clinging to it will be sufficient to steam it.

Transfer the spinach to a stockpot. Cover, and bring the spinach to a boil over medium heat; as soon as the boil is reached, season with salt and stir the spinach with a wooden spoon. Turn off the heat, transfer the spinach to a colander, and run cold water over it. Squeeze the spinach dry and chop coarsely.

In a mixing bowl, fold half the white sauce and half the grated cheese into the spinach. In another bowl, fold the remaining white sauce and cheese into the fish. Taste both mixtures and season with salt if necessary.

Ladle the spinach into a buttered deep 3-quart ovenproof baking dish and put the cod on top of the spinach. The dish can be prepared ahead of time up to this point; cover with buttered parchment paper and refrigerate overnight. Bring back to room temperature before baking.

Preheat the oven to 350 degrees.

Bake in the middle rack of the oven for 15 minutes; uncover and continue cooking for another 10 minutes or until the top bubbles and browns lightly. Serve immediately.

fricassee of shellfish

A fricassée (French), waterzooi (Belgian), or fricassee (English) belongs to the family of stews made with chicken or fish. The sauce is enriched with both cream and egg yolks or with only cream.

**SERVES 6
FOR A FIRST
COURSE, 4
FOR A MAIN
COURSE:**

18 littleneck clams
1 pound cockles, or more clams
1 pound mussels
1 pound sea scallops
2 tablespoons unsalted butter
$^1/_2$ cup minced shallots or onions
1 tablespoon minced garlic
1 14-ounce can Italian plum tomatoes, drained and chopped
$^1/_4$ cup minced parsley
$^1/_2$ cup heavy cream
Salt
Saffron Rice (page 119)

Soak the clams, cockles, and mussels in cold water for 10 minutes. Scrub them clean with a wire brush. Reserve, keeping each type of shellfish in a separate mixing bowl.

Quarter the sea scallops and reserve in a mixing bowl.

Melt the butter in a 5$^1/_2$-quart Dutch oven over medium-low heat. Stir in the shallots or onions, garlic, and 2 tablespoons water. Cover tightly and cook at a low simmer for 5 minutes, checking once in a while to be sure that the shallots or onions do not burn; if necessary, add more water.

Add the tomatoes, parsley, and cream. Cover and simmer gently for 15 minutes, stirring occasionally.

Raise the heat and add the littleneck clams and cockles. Cover and steam for 5 minutes; uncover and transfer the clams as they open to a colander set over a large mixing bowl. It will take about 10 minutes for all of them to open.

Add the mussels to the pot, cover tightly, and steam for 3 minutes or until the mussels open. Transfer the mussels to the bowl with the clams.

Lower the heat under the pot, and add the sea scallops to the broth. Cover tightly and poach the scallops at a gentle simmer for 4 to 5 minutes. Turn off the heat and cool the scallops in the broth.

When the clams and mussels have cooled, shell them over a mixing bowl to catch any liquor and add them to the sea scallops with the liquid in the bowl. With a large skimmer, transfer the shellfish to a heated bowl.

Raise the heat under the pot and boil down the cooking juices to about 1 cup or until very tasty (about 1 or 2 minutes). Season the sauce with salt if necessary. Pour over the shellfish and serve with saffron rice.

oyster chowder

This is a New England chowder made with oysters rather than the traditional clams. Buy oysters in the shell; shucked oysters sold in containers have lost most of their liquor, which is essential for the chowder. I take a large bowl with me to the fish market and ask the fishmonger to open the oysters above the bowl to catch the liquid that spews out and to leave them on the half-shell.

3 dozen large oysters on the half-shell

2 cups whole milk

1 teaspoon oil

3 ounces slab bacon, diced ($1/2$ cup)

1 leek, white part only, chopped medium-fine

1 large Yukon Gold potato, peeled and diced

2 tablespoons butter

2 tablespoons flour

$1/8$ teaspoon powdered saffron

SERVES 4 FOR A FIRST COURSE

Remove each oyster from its half-shell; strain the oyster liquor into a sieve lined with cheesecloth placed over a mixing bowl to trap any tiny fragments of shell, which should be discarded.

Put the oysters and liquor in a medium heavy-bottomed pot. Cover tightly and, over low to medium heat, bring slowly to a boil. Once the boil is reached, turn off the heat and let the oysters cool.

With a perforated ladle, scoop out the oysters and reserve for later. Strain the oyster liquid into a 4-cup measuring cup (you should have 1 cup liquid) and add enough milk to make 3 cups. Reserve.

In the same pot, heat the oil over medium heat and brown the bacon until light golden. Add the leeks and the potatoes with $1/4$ cup water and stir. Cover the pot and cook at a low simmer for 10 minutes, checking occasionally to make sure the leeks aren't burning. Add another $1/4$ cup of water if the vegetables stick to the bottom of the pot.

Meanwhile, melt the butter in a heavy-bottomed 2-quart pan, whisk in the flour until smooth, whisk in the oyster-milk mixture, and add the saffron. Cook over medium heat for 10 minutes, whisking occasionally.

Pour the white sauce over the potatoes and bacon. Cover and simmer over medium-low heat for 10 minutes or until the potatoes are tender. The chowder can be prepared ahead of time through this step.

To serve, reheat the chowder with the oysters over low heat until hot (about 5 minutes). The oyster liquor should be salty enough, but taste and adjust seasoning if necessary.

lobster stew

Large lobsters are at their best when they are braised at a slow simmer to keep the flesh moist. Years ago, I would go to Maine with friends to binge on lobster for a weekend. This dish is my interpretation of a stew I once had in a small diner there; it was so delicious, and in those days lobster was so cheap!

SERVES 4

1 cup white wine, preferably Chardonnay
1 medium onion, quartered, stuck with 4 cloves
6 fresh parsley stems
Salt
4 peppercorns
2 tablespoons butter
1 large leek, white part only, finely chopped (1^1/$_2$ cups)
1 large carrot, peeled and finely chopped (1 cup)
One 14-ounce can Italian plum tomatoes, drained and chopped
3 or 4 sprigs of fresh tarragon, finely chopped
^{1}/$_2$ teaspoon sugar
^{1}/$_8$ teaspoon crushed hot red pepper flakes
Freshly ground black pepper
One 3- to 4-pound live lobster
^{1}/$_2$ cup heavy cream
^{3}/$_4$ pound dried linguine
2 tablespoons olive oil
1 tablespoon lemon juice
1 tablespoon grated lemon peel

Combine 2 cups water, wine, onion, parsley, salt, and peppercorns in a 2-quart pot and bring slowly to a boil. Lower the heat and simmer for 30 minutes. Strain into a mixing bowl. This makes about 1 cup of broth (court bouillon).

Meanwhile, in a 7^1/$_4$-quart Dutch oven, combine butter, leeks, and carrots. Cover tightly and simmer gently over low heat for 15 minutes. Check once in a while to be sure that the leeks do not burn, and let the water that condenses under the lid fall back into the pot.

Stir in the tomatoes and the tarragon. Sprinkle with sugar, crushed pepper, salt, and freshly ground pepper. Cover tightly and continue simmering for another 10 minutes.

Uncover. Add the broth. Over the pot, twist off the lobster claws so any lobster liquor falls into the vegetables. Place the claws and the body of the lobster on top of the vegetables. Cover and simmer gently for 45 minutes, turning over the lobster pieces once in a while. As the lobster cooks, its liquor thickens to a light white custard that will blend into the vegetables.

Transfer the lobster to a colander and let cool. Wrap each claw in a towel and use a small hammer to break up the shell. Remove the meat and the "white custard" substance to a plate. Break off the body from the tail. With sturdy scissors, cut off the underside of the tail and remove the meat. Chop the lobster meat coarsely and mix it into the vegetables with the cream. Cover and reserve for later.

The lobster stew can be prepared ahead of time up to this stage.

Bring 5 quarts of salted water to a boil in a large pot. Cook the linguine to just under the al dente stage, about 5 minutes.

At the same time, reheat the lobster stew.

Drain the pasta and transfer to a large skillet with the oil, lemon juice, and grated peel. Over high heat, toss the linguine for several seconds.

Transfer the linguine to a heated platter and ladle the lobster stew over it.

waterzooi of mussels

A waterzooi is a Belgian seafood or chicken stew. It's a lovely first course for a dinner party, but it also can be served as a main course with boiled potatoes on the side.

3 pounds mussels
2 tablespoons butter
$1/3$ cup minced shallots or onions
$1/3$ cup diced carrots
$1/3$ cup diced white turnips
$1/3$ cup white wine, preferably Chardonnay
$1/3$ cup heavy cream
$1/8$ teaspoon saffron threads
2 egg yolks
Salt

Scrub the mussels clean with a wire brush under cold running water. Pull out the beards and discard any open mussels or any with broken shells.

Put the mussels into a large kettle, cover, and cook over high heat, shaking the pot until the mussels open, 2 to 3 minutes. Strain the mussel liquid through a double thickness of cheesecloth. This will make about 1 cup mussel liquid.

Shell the mussels and reserve the meat in a small bowl covered with a plate.

In a 4-quart Dutch oven, melt the butter over low heat. Add the shallots or onions and 2 tablespoons water. Cover and, over gentle heat, braise the shallots or onions for 5 minutes.

Add the carrots, turnips, mussel broth, wine, cream, and saffron strands. Bring to a boil, skim, cover, and simmer gently for 20 minutes. Strain the vegetables and reserve with the mussels. Set aside the braising liquid to cool.

In a small mixing bowl, whisk the egg yolks with $1/4$ cup of the braising liquid. Return the rest of the braising liquid to the Dutch oven, and whisk in the egg yolk mixture. Reheat slowly over gentle heat, stirring all the while; when the sauce is starting to thicken, add the mussels and vegetables. Whisk continuously over low heat, without bringing the stew to a boil, until the sauce takes on a creamy texture. Taste and add salt if necessary.

Serve in individual plates or ramekins for a first course, or serve with boiled potatoes if the waterzooi is your main dish.

cioppino

Portuguese fishermen who lived along the coast of California originally made this seafood chowder. This is my version, made with a spicy tomato sauce, to which I add white wine in lieu of red wine. I also use clams, shrimp, cod, and halibut instead of crab, lobster, and prawns, making the stew more affordable.

SERVES 6

$^1/_3$ cup olive oil
1 cup coarsely chopped onions
1 small green pepper, cored and finely diced
One 28-ounce can Italian plum tomatoes, coarsely chopped
1 tablespoon minced garlic
3 large sprigs of parsley, minced
$^1/_2$ teaspoon sugar
1 cup white wine, Chardonnay
$^1/_2$ teaspoon crushed red pepper flakes
3 dozen littleneck clams
$^1/_2$ pound skinned and boned cod, cut into 6 pieces
$^1/_2$ pound skinned and boned halibut, cut into 6 pieces
1 pound large unshelled shrimp
Salt, if necessary
Saffron Rice (page 119) or boiled potatoes

Heat the oil in a $7^1/_2$-quart Dutch oven; stir in the onion and green pepper. Cover and simmer over low to medium heat for 10 minutes. Uncover and add the chopped tomatoes and juice, garlic, parsley, sugar, and wine; sprinkle with red pepper flakes. Turn the heat to high and bring to a boil. Cover the pot, reduce the heat, and simmer for 45 minutes. The stew can be prepared ahead of time through this step.

Soak the clams in cold water for 15 minutes. Scrub them clean with a wire brush under cold running water. Reserve.

Reheat the tomato sauce and bring it to a boil. Add the cod and halibut, cover, and cook for 5 minutes over medium heat. Transfer the fish to a heated tureen; reserve in a warm oven.

Raise the heat under the pot; add the clams and unshelled shrimp. Cover and steam the clams and shrimp until the clams open and the shrimp turn bright red (about 3 minutes).

With a large perforated ladle, transfer the shellfish into the tureen with the cod and halibut. Keep in a warm oven.

Over high heat, bring the braising liquid in the pot to a boil and boil it down until very tasty—approximately to 1 to $1^1/_2$ cups, depending on the shellfish used. Taste, and adjust seasoning if necessary.

Ladle the sauce over the fish and shellfish in the soup tureen and serve immediately with saffron rice or boiled potatoes.

paella

Paella is a Spanish rice casserole made with chicken, pork, and seafood. It is one of the great dishes of the world. I consulted *The Foods and Wines of Spain*, a classic work by Penelope Casas, and was inspired by her Paella à la Valenciana.

You can use 1 large or 2 medium cast-iron skillets for the standard paella pan.

Traditional Paella contains snails that have feasted on rosemary; lacking that, Spaniards add rosemary.

SERVES 8

1 large red bell pepper
1 cup frozen peas
$1/2$ cup olive oil
8 chicken thighs, fat trimmed off
Salt
Freshly ground pepper
$1/4$ ounce prosciutto, diced
$1/4$ pound chorizo or garlic sausages, cut in $1/4$-inch-thick slices
$1/2$ pound pork chop, boned and diced
1 pound medium shrimp, shelled and deveined
1 cup coarsely chopped onion
1 cup coarsely chopped scallion greens
4 large garlic cloves, cut into slivers
3 cups short-grain rice
2 quarts Rich Chicken Stock (page 7)
$1/4$ teaspoon saffron threads
1 tablespoon lemon juice
2 bay leaves, crumbled
8 prawns or 16 large shrimp, not shelled
1 pound cockles or 16 soft-shell clams, scrubbed clean
1 pound mussels, scrubbed clean

Char the red pepper whole on top of the stove or under a broiler. Place it in a sturdy plastic bag and set aside to cool.

Peel the pepper and wash out the burned particles. Quarter the pepper and discard the seeds; cut each quarter into $1/4$-inch strips, then crosswise in $1/4$-inch cubes. Set aside.

Pour boiling water over the frozen peas. Drain and set aside.

Heat the oil in either one 13-inch or two 9-inch cast-iron skillets. Brown the chicken thighs over medium-high heat, skin side down first, turning them over when the skin side is golden brown. With tongs, transfer the chicken thighs to a platter; sprinkle with salt and freshly ground pepper. Set aside for later.

In the same oil, add the prosciutto, chorizo, and pork and brown for 5 minutes. With a wire-mesh ladle, transfer the meat to the chicken platter.

Add the shelled shrimp to the skillet, raise the heat, and stir-fry for 1 minute. Transfer the shrimp to the platter; set aside.

Add the onion, scallions, and garlic to the skillet, lower the heat, and cook for 2–3 minutes, stirring most of the time to prevent the onions and garlic from burning.

Add the rice to the skillet and stir until it is well coated with oil, onions, and garlic. At the same time bring the chicken broth to a boil with the saffron. Pour the broth over the rice and mix well; sprinkle with 1 tablespoon lemon juice, $1/2$ teaspoon salt, freshly ground pepper, and the crumbled bay leaf. Over medium heat, cook for 2 minutes, stirring occasionally.

Add the reserved red pepper, peas, chicken, meat, and shelled shrimp and mix into the rice; cover the skillet and set aside (the paella can be prepared ahead of time through this step).

Preheat the oven to 300 degrees.

Bake the paella in the middle of the oven for 20 minutes.

Meanwhile, bring 1 quart of water to a boil in a 4-quart pan and add the prawns or the shrimp. Boil until the shells are bright red. Drain and set aside in a warm place.

Put the cockles or clams and mussels into a large pot with no water. Cover the pot, adjust the heat to high, and steam the shellfish. As soon the cockles or clams and mussels open, remove them to a platter. Strain the liquid produced and reserve in a heated sauceboat.

Have a very large heated platter ready and spoon the rice and meats onto it. Stand the prawns, mussels, and clams in the rice. Serve the paella with the sauceboat of juices and individual finger bowls.

vegetables

Whenever my mother wanted me to eat vegetables, she felt she had to find ingenious ways to make them tasty. During World War II in occupied France, it was no mean feat to find butter, eggs, milk, or cream to transform vegetables into yummy creations. Years later, I married a man who had the same childhood problems with vegetables, especially with eggplant and zucchini. Eventually I discovered that his mother simply boiled these vegetables and set them down before him. The day I made Eggplant à la Napolitaine (page 149), he ate practically the entire dish by himself! And even though my taste is more sophisticated these days, I still love my childhood vegetable gratins. If you want to share my pleasure, try my favorite vegetable dish, Ratatouille, the quintessential vegetable stew (page 158).

All these vegetable dishes can be prepared in advance. If they're refrigerated, however, be sure to bring them back to room temperature before baking.